GCSE English

Romeo and Juliet

by William Shakespeare

Ever fallen in love with someone you shouldn't have fallen in love with?
Never mind — studying *Romeo & Juliet* will cheer you right up.

Better still, we've whipped up this brilliant CGP Workbook to help you score
top grades for your *R&J* essays. It's packed with practice questions to test your
knowledge of the plot, characters, themes, Shakespeare's techniques and more.

So settle down with this CGP book today — it may be a bit square,
but at least your family will probably approve.

The Workbook

CONTENTS

How to Use this Book 1

Section One — Analysis of Acts

Act One.. 2
Act Two 5
Act Three 8
Act Four... 11
Act Five 13
Skills Focus: Using Quotes 16
Skills Focus: P.E.E.D. 17

Section Two — Characters

Romeo... 18
Juliet.. 20
Mercutio.. 22
Tybalt & Benvolio 23
The Montagues 24
The Capulets.. 25
Nurse 26
Friar Lawrence 27
Paris, Prince & Others.. 28
Skills Focus: Making Links 29
Practice Questions.. 30

Section Three — Context and Themes

Religion... 31
Family and Marriage.. 32
Conflict, Honour and Feuds.. 34
Love 35
Fate 37
Skills Focus: Writing about Context 38
Practice Questions.. 39

CONTENTS

Section Four — Shakespeare's Techniques

Form and Structure of 'Romeo and Juliet'... 40
Mood and Atmosphere 42
Dramatic Irony 43
Poetry in Shakespeare.. 44
Puns and Wordplay 45
Imagery and Symbolism 46
Skills Focus: Working with Extracts 48
Practice Questions 49

Section Five — Exam Buster

Understanding the Question... 50
Making a Rough Plan 51
Making Links.. 52
Structuring Your Answer.. 53
Introductions and Conclusions 54
Writing about Context 55
Linking Ideas and Paragraphs... 56
Marking Answer Extracts... 57
Marking a Whole Answer 59
Skills Focus: Writing Well 61
Practice Questions.. 62

Answers... 63
The Characters from 'Romeo and Juliet'
'Romeo and Juliet' Cartoon

Published by CGP

Editors:
Rose Jones
Louise McEvoy
Liam Neilson
Jack Perry
Rebecca Tate

With thanks to Emma Crighton and Nicola Woodfin for the proofreading.
With thanks to Jan Greenway for the copyright research.

Acknowledgements:

Cover Image: Romeo and Juliet, 1884 (oil on canvas) by Dicksee, Sir Frank (1853-1928)
Southampton City Art Gallery, Hampshire, UK/ The Bridgeman Art Library.

With thanks to ArenaPAL for permission to use the images on pages 1, 19, 23, 36 and 43.

With thanks to Photostage for permission to use the images on pages 3, 5, 6, 9, 14, 24, 26, 28, 31, 34 and 46.

With thanks to Alamy for permission to use the images on pages 11, 13, 20, 27 and 33.

With thanks to Geraint Lewis for permission to use the images on pages 22, 25 and 45.

With thanks to Rex Features for permission to use the image on page 41.

ISBN: 978 1 78294 778 3

Printed by Elanders Ltd, Newcastle upon Tyne.

Clipart from Corel®

Based on the classic CGP style created by Richard Parsons.

Text, design, layout and original illustrations © Coordination Group Publications Ltd. (CGP) 2017

How to Use this Book

Practise the four main skills you'll need for the exam

Each question tests <u>one or more</u> of the <u>four skills</u> you'll be tested on in the <u>exam</u>. You'll need to:

1) Write about the text in a <u>thoughtful way</u>, <u>picking out</u> appropriate <u>examples</u> and <u>quotations</u> to back up your opinions.

2) <u>Identify</u> and <u>explain</u> features of the play's <u>form</u>, <u>structure</u> and <u>language</u>. Using <u>subject terminology</u>, show how the author uses these features to create <u>characters</u> and <u>settings</u>, explore <u>themes</u> and affect the <u>audience's reactions</u>.

3) Write about the play's <u>context</u> in your exam.

4) Write in a <u>clear</u>, <u>well-structured</u> and <u>accurate</u> way. <u>5%</u> of the marks in your English Literature GCSE are for <u>spelling</u>, <u>punctuation</u> and <u>grammar</u>.

Most exam boards will want you to write about context. Ask your teacher if you're not sure.

You can use this workbook with the CGP Text Guide

1) This book is perfect to use with CGP's <u>Text Guide</u> for *Romeo and Juliet*. It matches each <u>main section</u> of the Text Guide, so you can test your understanding of the play <u>bit by bit</u>.

2) The workbook tests all the <u>important</u> parts of the text that you'll need to know about for the exam — <u>plot</u>, <u>characters</u>, <u>context</u>, <u>themes</u> and <u>Shakespeare's techniques</u>.

3) The questions refer to the text <u>in detail</u> — you'll need a <u>copy</u> of the play to make the most of the workbook. The line numbers used throughout this book match CGP's <u>Romeo and Juliet — The Complete Play</u>.

© Royal Opera House/ArenaPAL

It prepares you for the exam every step of the way

1) The exam section is jam-packed with <u>useful advice</u>. It <u>guides</u> you through how to tackle the exam, from understanding the questions to building great answers. There's also an easy-to-read <u>mark scheme</u>, which you can use to mark <u>sample answers</u> and improve answers of your <u>own</u>.

2) There are four pages of <u>practice exam questions</u> spread across the book. They give you the opportunity to use what you've revised in each section to write a <u>realistic answer</u>.

3) <u>Exam tips</u> and extra <u>practice exam questions</u> are included throughout the book. There are also helpful <u>revision tasks</u> designed to get you thinking more creatively. These are marked with <u>stamps</u>.

4) You can find <u>answers</u> to all of the <u>questions</u> and <u>tasks</u> at the back of the book.

5) Each section contains at least one 'Skills Focus' page. These pages help you to practise important skills <u>individually</u>. You can tackle them in <u>any order</u> and prioritise the skills you find the <u>hardest</u>.

Think this looks promising? You ain't seen nothing Juli-yet...

Now you're clued-up on what this lovely book has to offer, it's time to leap head first into some questions. You're not in the exam just yet, so don't panic — just take your time and go through the book at your own pace.

Section One — Analysis of Acts

Act One

Act 1, Prologue — The whole story in fourteen lines

Q1 The Chorus mentions an "**ancient grudge**". What does this refer to?

....

Q2 Explain what Shakespeare means when he calls Romeo and Juliet "**a pair of star-crossed lovers**".

....

....

Act 1, Scene 1 — Romeo is lovesick

Q3 How does Sampson initially provoke the Montague servants?

....

Q4 Read lines 51-97 and decide whether each of the following statements is **true** or **false**.

	True	False
Benvolio doesn't want to fight Tybalt.	☐	☐
The citizens only join the fight to help the Capulets.	☐	☐
Lady Montague wants Montague to join the fighting.	☐	☐
The fight is Verona's first street brawl.	☐	☐
The Prince threatens to execute anyone who fights as part of the feud.	☐	☐

Q5 Read lines 165-192. How does Romeo feel in this passage? Explain why he feels this way.

....

....

....

Q6 According to Romeo, why won't Rosaline accept his love for her?

....

Act 1, Scene 2 — Capulet plans a party

Q1 Below are two reasons why Capulet thinks it is too early for Paris to marry Juliet. Find a quote to support each one.

a) Capulet believes Juliet is too young to marry.

Quote: ....

b) Paris must gain Juliet's consent first.

Quote: ....

Q2 Explain how Benvolio's reason for going to Capulet's party is different to Romeo's reason for going.

....

....

....

Act 1, Scene 3 — Juliet, Lady Capulet and the Nurse discuss marriage

Q3 What impression does the audience get of the Nurse in this scene? Give reasons for your answer.

....

....

....

....

© Donald Cooper/photostage

Q4 In your own words, describe what Lady Capulet thinks of Paris.

....

....

Q5 How does Juliet react to the news that Paris would like to marry her?

....

....

Section One — Analysis of Acts

Act 1, Scene 4 — Mercutio teases Romeo

Q1 Read Mercutio's speech about Queen Mab from line 53 to line 95.
Explain what the speech suggests about Mercutio's personality.

....

....

....

Q2 Why does Romeo feel worried about going to the party?

....

Act 1, Scene 5 — Romeo and Juliet fall in love at first sight

Q3 Put these events in order by numbering the boxes. The first one has been done for you.

Romeo sees Juliet for the first time and falls in love with her. ☐

Capulet tells Tybalt not to start fighting at the party. ☐

Romeo finds out that Juliet is a Capulet. ☐

Tybalt threatens to kill Romeo. ☐

Capulet welcomes the guests to the party. 1

Romeo kisses Juliet. ☐

Q4 Give two reasons why Capulet doesn't want Tybalt to fight Romeo at the party.

1) ....

2) ....

Q5 Towards the end of the scene, Juliet says: "**My only love
sprung from my only hate**". Explain what she means by this.

....

....

Paris, Rome(o) — Juliet has her pick of destinations...

Write Romeo's name at the centre of a sheet of paper. Around Romeo, write the names of Juliet,
Benvolio, Mercutio and Tybalt, with a sentence each that sums up how they feel towards Romeo so far.

Section One — Analysis of Acts

Act Two

Act 2, Prologue and Scene 1 — Benvolio and Mercutio can't find Romeo

Q1 How does the Prologue to Act Two suggest that Romeo and Juliet's love is dangerous?

....

....

Q2 Why does Mercutio call out rude sexual jokes to Romeo?

....

....

....

Act 2, Scene 2 — Juliet talks to Romeo from her window

Q3 Why does Juliet ask Romeo to reject his identity as a Montague?

....

....

Q4 Find a quote from this scene to back up each of these statements.

a) It is dangerous for Romeo to be in the orchard.

....

....

b) Juliet is embarrassed that she expressed her feelings so openly.

....

....

© Donald Cooper/photostage

Q5 Read lines 131-157. How do the stage directions in this passage influence the audience's impression of Romeo and Juliet's relationship at this point in the play?

....

....

....

Section One — Analysis of Acts

Act 2, Scene 3 — Romeo plans the wedding

Q1 Briefly describe the relationship between Romeo and Friar Lawrence in this scene. Use a quote to support your answer.

© Donald Cooper/photostage

....

....

....

....

....

Q2 Friar Lawrence has doubts about marrying Romeo and Juliet. Why do you think he feels this way?

....

....

Act 2, Scene 4 — Romeo tells the Nurse about his plan to marry Juliet

Q3 What new information does the audience learn at the start of the scene that may create problems for Romeo later in the play?

....

Q4 Read from line 35 to line 89. How is Romeo's behaviour here different to his behaviour in Act 1, Scene 4?

....

....

....

Q5 What does the Nurse think about Romeo marrying Juliet at this point in the play? Use a quote to support your answer.

....

....

Act 2, Scene 5 — Juliet learns of Romeo's plan

Q1 Find a quote from this scene to back up each of these statements.

  a) Juliet is anxious to hear what the Nurse has to say.

  ....

  b) The Nurse teases Juliet.

  ....

Q2 Read from line 66 to the end of the scene. In your own words, describe Romeo's plan.

  ....

  ....

  ....

  ....

Act 2, Scene 6 — Romeo and Juliet meet to get married

Q3 Friar Lawrence warns Romeo that "**These violent delights have violent ends**".
What does this suggest about later events in the play? Explain your answer.

  ....

  ....

Q4 Friar Lawrence says they "**will make short work**" of the wedding
ceremony. Why do you think he wants to finish the ceremony quickly?

  ....

  ....

Q5 Romeo and Juliet get married off stage. What effect does this create?

  ....

Revise the play and you'll make short work of the exam...

Imagine you're William Shakespeare and you've been asked by a friend what your new play,
Romeo and Juliet, is about. Write a paragraph summarising the first two acts to give them a taster.

Section One — Analysis of Acts

Act Three

Act 3, Scene 1 — Mercutio and Tybalt are killed

Q1 Why do you think Shakespeare creates a tense atmosphere at the beginning of this scene?

....

....

Q2 Put these events in order by numbering the boxes. The first one has been done for you.

Romeo, feeling angry, fights and kills Tybalt. ☐

Romeo places himself between Mercutio and Tybalt to try to end their fight. ☐

Tybalt approaches Mercutio and Benvolio, looking for Romeo. ☐ 1

Romeo runs away as the citizens arrive. ☐

Mercutio thinks Romeo is being a coward, and provokes Tybalt to fight him instead. ☐

Q3 Romeo is initially reluctant to fight with Tybalt and he doesn't want Mercutio to fight with him either. Why is this? Give two reasons.

1) ....

2) ....

Q4 Identify who said each of these phrases, then explain what each one means.

a) "A plague a'both your houses!" Said by: ....

Meaning: ....

....

b) "fire-eyed fury be my conduct now!" Said by: ....

Meaning: ....

....

Q5 The Prince only banishes Romeo from Verona, rather than executing him as he promised in Act One. Why do you think he does this?

....

....

Act 3, Scene 2 — Juliet gets some bad news

Q1 Read lines 35-68. Find a quote from this passage to back up each of these statements.

   a) Juliet believes Romeo is dead.

   Quote: ....

   b) The Nurse is distressed by Tybalt's death.

   Quote: ....

Q2 Juliet calls Romeo a "**Beautiful tyrant, fiend angelical!**" What does this tell you about Juliet's feelings towards Romeo at this point in the play? Explain your answer.

   ....

   ....

Q3 Read from line 97 to line 137. Explain how this passage shows Juliet's loyalty to Romeo. Use a quote to support your answer.

   ....

   ....

Act 3, Scene 3 — Romeo hears he's been banished

Q4 Explain how Romeo feels after hearing the news that he has been banished from Verona.

   ....

   ....

Q5 Read from line 136 to line 142. Summarise what Friar Lawrence says in this passage to convince Romeo not to act hastily.

© Donald Cooper/photostage

   ....

   ....

   ....

Q6 Why does Romeo's mood change at the end of the scene?

   ....

Section One — Analysis of Acts

Act 3, Scene 4 — Capulet agrees to Paris's proposal

Q1 Find a quote from this scene which shows that Capulet is confident that Juliet will obey him.

....

Q2 Why does Capulet only want a small wedding celebration?

....

Act 3, Scene 5 — Juliet refuses to marry Paris

Q3 Read lines 1-105 and decide whether each of the following statements is **true** or **false**. For each one, find a short quote to support your answer.

a) Juliet is glad that it is morning.   **True:** ☐   **False:** ☐

Quote: ....

b) Lady Capulet believes Juliet is crying because of Tybalt's death.   **True:** ☐   **False:** ☐

Quote: ....

c) Lady Capulet presents the wedding positively to Juliet.   **True:** ☐   **False:** ☐

Quote: ....

Q4 How does Capulet's treatment of Juliet in this scene create sympathy for her from the audience? Use a quote to support your answer.

....

....

....

Q5 Why does Juliet feel betrayed when the Nurse says she should marry Paris?

....

....

Capulet forgot 'forever hold your peace' is the vicar's line...

Imagine you're a detective in Verona investigating Mercutio's death. Choose three factors from earlier in the play that contributed to his death, then write a few sentences for each explaining the effect it had.

     ☐   ☐   ☐

Act Four

Act 4, Scene 1 — Friar Lawrence has a plan for Juliet

Q1 How does Juliet speak to Paris in this scene? Use a quote to support your answer.

....

....

Q2 Why do you think Friar Lawrence tries so hard to help Juliet?

....

....

© AF archive / Alamy Stock Photo

Act 4, Scenes 2 and 3 — Juliet tricks her parents, then drinks the potion

Q3 Capulet starts to prepare the wedding without Juliet's consent.
What does this show about his attitude towards Juliet?

....

Q4 Why do you think Capulet decides to move the wedding forward by a day?

....

Q5 At the start of Scene 3, how does Juliet make sure that she will be alone for the rest of the night?

....

....

Q6 Read from line 36 to the end of Scene 3. Explain how this passage
shows Juliet's determination to carry out Friar Lawrence's plan.

....

....

Act 4, Scene 4 — The Capulet household prepares for the wedding

Q1 How can you tell that Capulet and Lady Capulet are in a good mood in this scene?

....

Q2 Why might the audience feel tense at the end of this scene?

....

....

Act 4, Scene 5 — The Capulets, the Nurse and Paris mourn Juliet

Q3 How does the Nurse's reaction to finding Juliet's dead body show that she loved Juliet?

....

Q4 Explain what Capulet means when he says that "**Death is my heir**".

....

....

Q5 Explain how the audience's attitude towards Lady Capulet
changes in this scene. Use a quote to support your answer.

....

....

....

Q6 Friar Lawrence encourages the Capulets to begin the funeral
as soon as possible. Why do you think he does this?

....

....

It's a good job Capulet only invited half a dozen friends...

Write the Friar's letter to Romeo, explaining his plan. In your letter, include anything relevant that's
happened since Romeo left for Mantua, what Juliet plans to do and what Romeo should do next.

Section One — Analysis of Acts

Act Five

Act 5, Scene 1 — Romeo thinks Juliet is dead

Q1 How does Romeo's dream at the start of the scene create an ominous atmosphere?

....

....

Q2 When Romeo decides to return to Verona, Balthasar tells him to **"have patience"**. Do you think Romeo is right to ignore his advice? Use information from the play so far in your answer.

....

....

....

Q3 Find a quote from the scene that describes the apothecary's appearance.

....

Q4 Read Romeo's conversation with the apothecary on lines 57-84. How does Romeo convince the apothecary to sell him the poison?

....

....

Act 5, Scene 2 — The Friar finds out his message hasn't reached Romeo

Q5 Why couldn't Friar John deliver Friar Lawrence's letter to Romeo?

....

....

Q6 What two things does Friar Lawrence plan to do when he realises his letter hasn't been delivered?

1) ....

2) ....

Section One — Analysis of Acts

Act 5, Scene 3 — Romeo kills Paris, then kills himself

Q1 Read the paragraph below and fill in the gaps using words from the box.

Paris arrives to place .... at Juliet's tomb. Romeo then arrives

and tells .... not to disturb him while he is in the tomb. Paris

sees Romeo, and identifies him as a member of the ....

family. He approaches Romeo with the intention of .... him.

Paris
Montague
killing
Balthasar
arresting
torches
Capulet
flowers

Q2 Read lines 1-21. Find a quote that suggests Paris loves Juliet.

....

Q3 Why does Paris assume that Romeo wants to vandalise the tomb?

....

....

....

Q4 Find a quote which shows that Romeo does not want to fight Paris. Explain how it shows this.

Quote: ....

Explanation: ....

....

Q5 Read lines 88-120. Why is this part of the scene tense for the audience?

....

....

....

....

Section One — Analysis of Acts

Act 5, Scene 3 continued — Juliet dies and everyone learns the truth

Q1 Which of the following best describe Juliet's reaction to waking up and finding out that Romeo is dead? Tick **two** boxes.

She accepts Romeo's death and is determined to die too. ☐

She is frustrated that she did not wake up sooner. ☐

She is initially confused that Romeo is not there to greet her. ☐

Q2 Read lines 161-170. Why do you think Shakespeare creates similarities between this passage and the dream Romeo has in Act 5, Scene 1?

....

....

....

Q3 Put these events in order by numbering the boxes. The first one has been done for you.

The Prince arrives, followed by Capulet and Lady Capulet. ☐

The watchmen find the dead bodies in the tomb. ☐ 1

Balthasar gives Romeo's letter to the Prince. ☐

Montague arrives at the tomb and reveals his wife has died. ☐

Friar Lawrence explains the events leading up to Romeo and Juliet's deaths. ☐

The watchmen find Balthasar and Friar Lawrence in the churchyard. ☐

Q4 Read Friar Lawrence's speech to the Prince, the Montagues and the Capulets on lines 229-269. What does it reveal about his character? Explain your answer.

....

....

....

....

Q5 Give one positive consequence of Romeo and Juliet's deaths.

....

Juliet didn't wake up in time — it was a cause for alarm...

Make a timeline of the main events of the play, including the day that each event happens on.
To start you off, the play begins on Sunday and ends on Thursday morning. Now, fill in the rest.

Section One — Analysis of Acts

Using Quotes

In the exam, you'll have to back up your points with quotes from the play. You won't have a copy of the text with you, so it's important to memorise some useful quotes. To really impress the examiner, you'll need to embed your quotes in your sentences so that they sound natural. This means picking out the parts of your quote that are the most relevant to your point and then including them in a sentence to back up that point. Have a go at these questions and you'll get the hang of it in no time.

Q1 Read these statements about quotes. Decide whether each one is **true** or **false**.

	True	False
All your quotes should be written exactly as they appear in the text.	☐	☐
An embedded quote is better than a quote added to the end of a sentence.	☐	☐
Quotes should simply repeat what you have written.	☐	☐
You should include lots of long quotes.	☐	☐
Your quotes don't necessarily need to back up your argument.	☐	☐

Q2 Rewrite the following sentences so that a short part of the quote is embedded in each one. The first one has been done for you.

Sentence	Quote	New sentence
a) Montague wishes he could solve his son's problems.	"Could we but learn from whence his sorrows grow, / We would as willingly give cure as know."	Montague wishes he could "give cure" to his son's problems.
b) Romeo thinks that Juliet is so radiant that he calls her an angel.	"She speaks. / O speak again, bright angel"	
c) In Act One, the Prince thinks that the people who started the fight are disgraceful.	"Where are the vile beginners of this fray?"	
d) Paris explains that Capulet has moved Juliet's marriage forward to comfort her.	"And in his wisdom hastes our marriage / To stop the inundation of her tears"	
e) Romeo can't see any sign of death in Juliet's face.	"And death's pale flag is not advancèd there."	

P.E.E.D.

P.E.E.D. is a great way for you to structure your answers — it makes your paragraphs more concise and analytical. In each of your paragraphs, you need to make a **point**, give a supporting **example**, then **explain** how this example backs up your argument. Finally, to really impress the examiner, you need to **develop** your point by explaining its effect on the audience, or its links to themes, context or other events in the play. Here are a couple of exercises to help you get to grips with P.E.E.D.

Q1 Neither of the sample answers below have used P.E.E.D. correctly.
For each, say which stage of P.E.E.D. is missing.

a)

> Tybalt is established as a violent character right from Act 1, Scene 1, in which he claims to "hate the word" 'peace'. Tybalt's aggressive nature is confirmed later in the play when he challenges Romeo to a duel and fatally wounds Mercutio.

Missing stage: ....

b)

> Shakespeare suggests that fate, rather than the characters, controls the action of the play. When Romeo realises the consequences of killing Tybalt, he says "O, I am fortune's fool." This shows that Romeo feels he is being controlled by fate as a king might control his "fool" or jester.

Missing stage: ....

Q2 Fill in the missing steps in the P.E.E.D. structures below.

a) Point: Shakespeare suggests that Romeo's love for Rosaline is not genuine.

Example: Friar Lawrence accuses Romeo of "doting" on Rosaline rather than "loving" her.

Explain: ....
....

Develop: This contrasts with the way Shakespeare presents Romeo's true love for Juliet.

b) Point: Mercutio is presented as a vulgar character in some parts of the play.

Example: ....

Explain: Here, Mercutio refers to Romeo's love for Rosaline using sexual puns.

Develop: Mercutio's use of vulgar language adds humour to the scene.

    Section One — Analysis of Acts

Section Two — Characters

Romeo

Q1 Fill in the gaps in the table below. The first one has been done for you.

What Romeo does	What it reveals about Romeo
a) Romeo says that his sorrow at being unloved by Rosaline has made him into a different man.	Romeo is easily swept up by his emotions.
b) He goes to Capulet's party to see Rosaline, even though she's said she isn't interested in him.	
c) Romeo claims he is deeply in love with Rosaline, then forgets his love for her when he meets Juliet.	
d) Romeo climbs into the Capulets' orchard to see Juliet, after only just meeting her.	
e) He jokes with Mercutio and Benvolio.	

Q2 How does Romeo's opinion of love change when he's in love with Juliet? Use a quote to support your answer.

....

....

....

Q3 Find a quote from Act 2, Scene 4 which suggests that Romeo's emotions change as a result of meeting Juliet.

....

Q4 In Act 3, Scene 3, Friar Lawrence scolds Romeo, telling him "**thou sham'st thy shape, thy love, thy wit.**" State what this quote means and explain what it suggests about Romeo's behaviour in this scene.

Meaning: ....

Explanation: ....

....

Q5 Find a quote from the play which shows Romeo is:

© Bill Cooper/ArenaPAL

a) emotional

Quote: ....

b) strong-willed

Quote: ....

c) polite

Quote: ....

Q6 Why do you think Shakespeare presents Romeo as a peaceful character at the start of the play?

....

....

....

Q7 In Act 3, Scene 1, Romeo says that his love for Juliet has "**softened**" his courage.
Do you think this is true? Refer to the events in Act 3, Scene 1 in your answer.

....

....

....

....

Q8 Briefly describe Romeo's emotions in Act 5, Scene 1. Use a quote to support your answer.

....

....

....

....

(EXAM PRACTICE)

Romeo — romantic hero or obsessive stalker?...

Read Act 3, Scene 3, lines 100-123, then answer the following question. **'Throughout the play, Romeo is shown to be passionate.'** **Explain how Romeo is presented as a passionate character in the extract and in the rest of *Romeo and Juliet*.** Remember to support your points with evidence.

Section Two — Characters

Juliet

Q1 Find a quote from the play that shows that Juliet is:

a) impulsive

Quote: ....

b) practical

Quote: ....

c) impatient

Quote: ....

Q2 Juliet tells Romeo that their love is "**too rash, too unadvised, too sudden**" (Act 2, Scene 2, line 118). What does this suggest about the way Juliet views love?

....

....

....

Q3 Read Act 4, Scene 1, lines 77-88. How does Juliet's language in this passage show her unwillingness to marry Paris? Use a quote to back up your answer.

....

....

....

Q4 In Act 4, Scene 1, Juliet is willing to go along with Friar Lawrence's plan, despite how dangerous it could be. Do you think this shows that Juliet is brave or foolish? Explain your answer.

....

....

....

....

Q5 In Act 2, Scene 2, Juliet is preoccupied by Romeo's identity as a Montague and the problems it might cause for her as a Capulet. Explain how her attitude to her family has changed by Act 3, Scene 5.

....

....

....

Q6 Decide whether these statements about Juliet are **true** or **false**.

	True	False
Juliet says she feels nervous about meeting Paris. (Act 1, Scene 3)	☐	☐
Juliet is confident that Romeo will arrange the wedding. (Act 2, Scene 5)	☐	☐
Juliet is excited about her wedding night. (Act 3, Scene 2)	☐	☐
Juliet tells Paris she does not want to marry him. (Act 4, Scene 1)	☐	☐

Q7 In Act 1, Scene 3, Lady Capulet and the Nurse state that Juliet is only 13 years old. Why might her age make an audience feel sorry for her?

....

....

....

....

Q8 In Act 3, Scene 5, Juliet refuses to marry Paris as she is secretly married to Romeo. Do you think this shows that Juliet is a moral character? Explain your answer.

....

....

....

....

Mercutio

Q1 Give two ways in which Mercutio's personality is different to Romeo's personality.

1) ....

2) ....

Q2 Find a quote that supports each of the following statements.

a) The Nurse thinks Mercutio is rude.

Quote: ....

b) Romeo thinks Mercutio enjoys attention.

Quote: ....

c) Benvolio thinks Mercutio is courageous.

Quote: ....

Q3 Give one reason that Mercutio's friendship with Romeo is important to the play's plot, then explain your answer.

....

....

Q4 How does Mercutio's personality help to create conflict in Act 3, Scene 1? Use a quote to support your answer.

....

....

....

....

....

© Geraint Lewis

EXAM TIP

When Mercutio dies, so do the jokes — tragic...

Mercutio's death is a big turning point in the play. His character introduces lots of comedy to the play, so when he dies it becomes much more serious. Make sure you know the scene well.

Tybalt & Benvolio

Q1   Find two quotes from the play which suggest that Benvolio tries to avoid conflict.

1) ....

2) ....

Q2   Briefly describe an event in the play in which Tybalt is:

a) reckless

Event: ....

....

b) persistent

Event: ....

....

Q3   Read lines 148-171 of Act 3, Scene 1. What information does Benvolio leave out when he describes the fight to the Prince? Explain what this suggests about his character.

....

....

....

....

Q4   In Act 3, Scene 2, the Nurse says that Tybalt was **"the best friend I had"**.
What can the audience learn about Tybalt's character from this quote?

....

....

Tybalt and Mercutio were fighting like cat and dog...

Mercutio compares Tybalt to a fictional character called 'Prince of Cats', and Benvolio's name means 'good will'. Write a paragraph for each of them, explaining how these names reflect their personalities.

The Montagues

Q1 Read lines 73-74 of Act 1, Scene 1. What do they reveal about the personalities of Montague and Lady Montague?

Montague: ....

Lady Montague: ....

Q2 Find a quote from Act 1, Scene 1 that supports each of the following statements.

a) Montague is concerned about Romeo's gloomy mood.

Quote: ....

b) Montague hasn't been able to find out what's wrong with Romeo.

Quote: ....

Q3 What does the nature of Lady Montague's death suggest about her personality? Explain your answer.

....

....

....

Q4 How is Montague's behaviour after the deaths of Romeo and Juliet different to his behaviour following the deaths of Mercutio and Tybalt? Use quotes to support your answer.

....

....

....

....

....

© Donald Cooper/photostage

I'd write more, but I don't have a Monta-clue...

PRACTICE TASK

Some people think that Montague and Lady Montague are less responsible for the feud than Capulet and Lady Capulet. Do you agree with this view? Write a paragraph explaining your answer.

The Capulets

Q1 Fill in the gaps in the table below. The first one has been done for you.

Event in the play	What it suggests about Lady Capulet
a) Lady Capulet ensures the Nurse is in the room when she speaks to Juliet.	Lady Capulet is uncomfortable at being left alone with Juliet.
b) Lady Capulet enthusiastically describes Paris's noble qualities to Juliet.	
c) Lady Capulet offers to help Juliet get ready for her wedding to Paris.	

Q2 Why do you think Shakespeare presents Capulet as a caring father in Act 1, Scene 2?

....

....

Q3 Read lines 69-92 of Act 3, Scene 5. What does Lady Capulet's reaction to Juliet's sadness reveal about her character?

© Geraint Lewis

....

....

....

Q4 Find a quote from Act 4, Scene 4 which suggests that Capulet is excited about Juliet's wedding.

....

Q5 Read lines 126-195 of Act 3, Scene 5. How does Capulet's language suggest he is used to being obeyed by Juliet? Give a quote to support your answer.

....

....

....

EXAM TIP

Time to get your thinking Capulet on...

Capulet's character is one of the more interesting ones in the play. When writing about him, remember to include his caring side in Act 1, as well as his controlling side at the end of Act 3.

Nurse

Q1 Find two quotes that show that the Nurse acts as a motherly figure to Juliet.

1) ....

2) ....

Q2 Read lines 21-77 of Act 2, Scene 5. What does the humour in this passage suggest about the Nurse?

....

....

Q3 What role does the Nurse play in Romeo and Juliet's relationship? Explain why it is necessary for her to play this role.

....

....

....

© Donald Cooper/photostage

Q4 In Act 3, Scene 5, the Nurse tells Juliet to marry Paris. Why is this significant? Use a quote to support your answer.

....

....

....

Q5 In Act 5, Scene 3, the Prince says that some characters will be "**punishèd**" for Romeo and Juliet's death. Do you think the Nurse should be punished? Explain your answer.

....

....

MAKING LINKS

It's easy to lose patients with the Nurse...

The Nurse links to the theme of family. She's the Capulets' servant, but she raised Juliet so she's more like a mother to her than Lady Capulet — she's arguably a better parent than Juliet's actual parents.

Section Two — Characters

Friar Lawrence

Q1   Friar Lawrence agrees to marry Romeo to Juliet because he hopes that their marriage might turn their "**households' rancour**" into "**pure love.**" Explain what this suggests about Friar Lawrence.

....

....

Q2   Read Act 2, Scene 6. Find two quotes from this scene which show that Friar Lawrence is wise.

1) ....

2) ....

Q3   In Act 2, Scene 3, Friar Lawrence warns Romeo that "**they stumble that run fast**". Explain how this quote could apply to Friar Lawrence's own actions in the play and their consequences.

....

....

....

Q4   Give an event from the play which suggests that Friar Lawrence is cowardly.

....

Q5   Find a quote from Act 3, Scene 3 which shows that Friar Lawrence is a respected figure. Explain how it shows this.

....

....

....

....

© AF archive / Alamy Stock Photo

Fry a Lawrence? This play's even darker than I thought...

PRACTICE TASK

Friar Lawrence has negative traits, as well as positive ones. Make a list of his negative qualities, using evidence to support your choices. Your list shouldn't repeat any qualities identified on this page.

Paris, Prince & Others

Q1 Find a quote from the play which shows that Paris is:

a) determined

Quote: ....

b) respectful

Quote: ....

Q2 Read lines 18-43 of Act 4, Scene 1. Do you think Paris behaves kindly or arrogantly towards Juliet in this passage? Explain your choice.

....

....

....

Q3 How does the Prince's language suggest he is a figure of authority in the play? Give a quote to support your answer.

....

....

....

....

....

© Donald Cooper/photostage

Q4 Who do you think is a more important character in the play, Balthasar or Peter? Explain your answer.

....

....

....

EXAM TIP

I was rooting for the servants, but their role Petered out...

Minor characters are used by Shakespeare at crucial moments of the play. They are always included for a reason, so take some time to think about why a certain character appears at a particular moment.

Section Two — Characters

Making Links

A really good way to improve your answers is to make links between your point and different parts of the play. You can do this in lots of different ways, including making links between characters, events or themes. This page will get you thinking about how some of the main characters behave in different parts of the play. Try to only use specific examples — it'll make your points much more convincing.

Q1 Fill in the table below with examples to illustrate the key points about each character. You can either use quotes or just explain what happens, as long as it's a precise example.

Character	Key Point	Example One	Example Two
Romeo	Romeo is a romantic character.		
Juliet	Juliet behaves impulsively.		
Nurse	The Nurse is affectionate towards Juliet.		

Q2 Now do the same for the characters below. This time, you'll need to think of your own key point about them.

Character	Key Point	Example One	Example Two
Mercutio			
Tybalt			
Benvolio			

Section Two — Characters

Practice Questions

Well, now you know your Benvolio from your Balthasar and your Montague from your Capulet, it's time to get down to business and answer some practice questions. There are four of them below, each testing your knowledge of characters. Give them a try, and remember to write a plan before starting each answer.

Q1 To what extent is the Nurse presented as irresponsible? In your answer, refer to the extract below from Act 2, Scene 4 and to the play as a whole.

Nurse:	Now, afore God, I am so vexed, that every part about me quivers. Scurvy knave! Pray you, sir, a word — and as I told you, my young lady bid me enquire you out; what she bid me say, I will keep to myself. But first let me tell ye, if ye should lead her into a fool's paradise, as they say, it were a very gross kind of behaviour, as they say: for the gentlewoman is young; and, therefore, if you should deal double with her, truly it were an ill thing to be offered to any gentlewoman, and very weak dealing.
Romeo:	Nurse, commend me to thy lady and mistress. I protest unto thee —
Nurse:	Good heart, and, i'faith, I will tell her as much. Lord, Lord, she will be a joyful woman.
Romeo:	What wilt thou tell her, Nurse? Thou dost not mark me.
Nurse:	I will tell her, sir, that you do protest — which, as I take it, is a gentlemanlike offer.
Romeo:	Bid her devise Some means to come to shrift this afternoon; And there she shall at Friar Lawrence' cell Be shrived and married. Here is for thy pains.
Nurse	No truly sir, not a penny.
Romeo:	Go to, I say you shall.
Nurse:	This afternoon, sir? Well, she shall be there.

(Act 2, Scene 4, lines 142-165)

Q2 Read Act 3, Scene 2, lines 71-101, then answer the questions below.

a) How does Shakespeare present Juliet in this extract?

b) In this extract, Juliet shows loyalty to Romeo, despite the fact he has killed Tybalt. What is the significance of loyalty between characters in the rest of *Romeo and Juliet*? You should consider:

- times when characters show loyalty to each other
- how loyalty influence events in the play.

Q3 Read Act 3, Scene 4, lines 1-29. Explain how Shakespeare presents Capulet in this extract and in the rest of the play.

Q4 Read Act 3, Scene 1, lines 70-90. How is Mercutio presented as arrogant in the play? Refer to the extract and to the play as a whole.

Section Two — Characters

Religion

Q1 Complete this paragraph about religion in the play.

© Donald Cooper/photostage

Romeo and Juliet live in a very religious society. In the play, the

characters take the moral .... set out by their

religion very .... Couples always got married in a

.... and didn't usually live together before their

.... This is why marriage is the ....

way that Romeo and Juliet can properly be ....·

Q2 Fill in the table below to show how each idea about religion affects an event in the play.

Idea about religion in the play	How it affects an event in the play
a) It was considered a sin to have more than one husband or wife.	Juliet would be committing a sin by marrying Paris because she has already married Romeo, so she goes to Friar Lawrence for help.
b) People who worked for the Church were seen as very trustworthy.	
c) It was viewed as a sin to kill yourself.	

Q3 Read Act 3, Scene 5, lines 204-234. Do you think the Nurse cares that Juliet would be committing a sin by marrying Paris? Use a quote to support your answer.

....

....

....

Q4 Shakespeare sets the play in Italy, a mostly Catholic society. Catholics believe confessing their sins helps them to be forgiven. Give one way that confession is important in the play.

....

Include context religiously and you won't go far wrong...

When you're planning out your answer in the exam, note down where you could include some information about the play's context — just make sure it's relevant to the question you're being asked.

Family and Marriage

Q1 Shakespeare presents families both positively and negatively in *Romeo and Juliet*. Find a quote to back up each of these statements.

    a) Family members often offer each other support.

    ....

    b) Families can be a source of pressure.

    ....

Q2 Capulet is the head of his family. Describe two events when he shows this authority in the play.

    1) ....

    2) ....

Q3 Juliet is Capulet's only child. How might this have affected Capulet's choice of husband for her?

    ....

    ....

    ....

Q4 Find a quote said by each of the following characters which suggests they are trying to be loyal to their family.

    a) Juliet

    ....

    b) Tybalt

    ....

Q5 How does the way Paris courts Juliet conform to social expectations about marriage in the 16th century?

    ....

    ....

Q6   Read Act 1, Scene 3. How does Lady Capulet's own
experience of marriage influence how she treats Juliet?

....

....

....

....

© AF archive / Alamy Stock Photo

Q7   Why would Juliet's refusal to marry Paris have been seen as more rebellious
in the 16th century than it would be considered now? Explain your answer.

....

....

....

....

Q8   Find a quote which suggests that Juliet's position within her family restricts her freedom.

....

Q9   Read Act 3, Scene 1, from line 138 to the end of the scene. Then answer the following questions.

a) Do you think the Prince's family ties to Mercutio influence his decision
to banish Romeo, rather than execute him? Explain your answer.

....

....

....

b) Find another example in this passage which shows that family is
important to the play. Explain how your example shows this.

Quote: ....

Explanation: ....

....

PRACTICE TASK

Romeo and Juliet — a marriage made in heaven...

Pretend you're the lovesick Romeo. Write a letter to Capulet in which you ask his permission to
marry Juliet. Try to use the kind of arguments a 16th-century father would have found convincing.

Section Three — Context and Themes

Conflict, Honour and Feuds

Q1 Many people in England in the 16th century associated Italians with passion and conflict. How are these stereotypes shown in the feud between the Montague and Capulet families?

....

....

....

Q2 Why do you think Shakespeare chose to start the play with a fight?

....

....

....

Q3 The following statements are about the feud between the Montague and Capulet families. Tick the statements that are **true**.

The conflict is just between the upper-class characters.

The two sides look for opportunities to provoke one another.

Having a strong sense of family honour makes the feud worse.

The feud only affects the Montagues and the Capulets.

© Donald Cooper/photostage

Q4 Read Act 3, Scene 1, lines 53-90. In this passage, how does honour conflict with Romeo's desire to be with Juliet? Explain your answer.

....

....

....

Q5 Read Act 5, Scene 3, from line 286 to the end of the scene. Why does the feud end?

....

Feu, thank goodness that conflict's all sorted out now...

Read Act 1, Scene 5, lines 53-75. Write an essay plan for this question: **Explore the significance of the theme of honour in *Romeo and Juliet*. In your answer, you should refer to the passage and the rest of the play.** When writing your plan, back up your ideas with examples from the text.

Section Three — Context and Themes

Love

Q1 Explain how Romeo's love for Juliet is different to his love for Rosaline.

....

....

....

....

Q2 Explain how the relationship between Romeo and Rosaline reflects the aspects of courtly love listed below. Include a quote in each of your explanations.

Courtly love was a medieval tradition of love between a knight and his beloved.

Aspect of courtly love	How it's reflected in Romeo and Rosaline's relationship
a) Being in love is a painful experience for the man.	
b) The man's love is usually unrequited (unreturned).	
c) Love seems full of contradictions.	

Q3 In Act 2, Scene 3, Friar Lawrence talks to Romeo about his love for Rosaline, saying **"she knew well / Thy love did read by rote and could not spell"** (lines 87-88). Explain what this quote means, referring to words from the quote in your answer.

....

....

....

Q4 Read lines 92-109 of Act 1, Scene 5. How does Shakespeare use rhyme in this passage to show that Romeo and Juliet have fallen in love?

....

....

....

Q5 Shakespeare shows different sides to Romeo and Juliet's love.
Find a quote to back up each of the following statements.

a) Romeo feels true love for Juliet.

....

b) Juliet feels sexual desire for Romeo.

....

Q6 Juliet chooses to marry for love. Why would this have
been unusual at the time Shakespeare was writing?

....

....

Q7 Find a quote in which the Nurse jokes about sexual love. Explain
why you think Shakespeare includes rude jokes about sex in the play.

Quote: ....

Explanation: ....

....

....

Q8 How does Shakespeare link love to death in the play?

....

....

....

....

MAKING LINKS

I tried to woo a judge with poetry — it was courtly love...

Without love, *Romeo and Juliet* would be pretty boring. Think about the different types of love
Shakespeare presents to the audience, and how love links to themes like family, marriage and conflict.

Section Three — Context and Themes

Fate

Q1 How does the Act 1 Prologue suggest that Romeo and Juliet are fated to die? Use quotes to support your answer.

....

....

Q2 Find two quotes which suggest that Romeo believes in fate.

1) ....

2) ....

Q3 'Juliet's choices are the main cause of her and Romeo's deaths.'
Do you agree with this statement? Give a reason for your answer.

....

....

....

Q4 Give one way that fate is shown to be a powerful force in the play.

....

....

Q5 It isn't always clear whether fate controls the events in the play, or whether the characters are in control of their own destinies. Why do you think Shakespeare makes it unclear?

....

....

It's probably my fate to keep procrastinating — isn't it?...

Read Act 1, Scene 4, lines 96-114. **Explain how the theme of fate is significant in *Romeo and Juliet*.**
You should write about this extract and the rest of the play. You should consider:

- how Shakespeare presents fate in this extract
- how fate affects the play as a whole.

Section Three — Context and Themes

Writing about Context

To get a high mark in the exam, you'll need to discuss the context of *Romeo and Juliet*. The play was written in the 16th century, when attitudes towards things like love and marriage were stricter than they are today. It's important to show the examiner that you understand how context might have influenced Shakespeare when he was writing the play and how it might affect different audiences.

Q1 Read the sample answer extracts below and underline the contextual information.

> **a)** Shakespeare presents Capulet as the head of his family. When Juliet refuses to marry Paris, her father issues commands such as "Speak not, reply not, do not answer". This string of imperatives prevents Juliet from speaking, demonstrating Capulet's belief that as her father, he has the right to control her. The idea that the father should be the authority figure within the family would have been familiar to an audience in the 16th century, and would have made Juliet's decision to marry Romeo without her parent's permission seem more rebellious.

> **b)** The themes of love and marriage are closely linked in *Romeo and Juliet*. In Act 2, Scene 2, in which Romeo and Juliet express their love for one another, Juliet asks Romeo to "be honourable" and marry her, despite the fact that they have only known each other for a day. This suggests that Juliet believes they would be wrong to continue their relationship without being married. Juliet's insistence on marriage may have made their relationship seem more legitimate to the audience; in Shakespeare's time, many people would have considered it sinful for an unmarried couple to live or sleep together.

Q2 The bullet points below form the first three parts of a P.E.E.D. paragraph (see p.17). Read through them and choose the most appropriate piece of context from the numbered list to develop the paragraph. Then write a short explanation of how your chosen piece of context relates to the rest of the paragraph.

> * Religion is shown to be a powerful force in *Romeo and Juliet*.
> * Juliet tells Friar Lawrence she is "past hope, past cure, past help" when it appears that she will have to go against her religion by being married to both Paris and Romeo.
> * The repetition of the word "past" emphasises to the audience how bad Juliet believes her situation to be.

1) Suicide was considered an immoral act in Shakespeare's time.

2) At the time, many people believed that marriage was a sacred agreement with God, so it was important that nothing happened to make it less holy.

3) In the 16th century, most people were religious and attended church every Sunday.

Piece of context: ....

Explanation of choice: ....

....

....

Section Three — Context and Themes

Practice Questions

Here are some delightful exam-style questions to tickle your taste buds. Don't rush them — take five minutes or so to plan each answer and use the P.E.E.D. method (see p.17) to explain your ideas clearly.

Q1 Explain how different attitudes towards love are presented in the play.
Refer to the extract below and to the play as a whole.

Mercutio:	Romeo! Humours! Madman! Passion! Lover!
	Appear thou in the likeness of a sigh,
	Speak but one rhyme, and I am satisfied.
	Cry but 'Ay me!' pronounce but 'love' and 'dove',
	Speak to my gossip Venus one fair word,
	One nickname for her purblind son and heir,
	Young Adam Cupid, he that shot so trim,
	When King Cophetua loved the beggar-maid!
	He heareth not, he stirreth not, he moveth not;
	The ape is dead, and I must conjure him.
	I conjure thee by Rosaline's bright eyes,
	By her high forehead and her scarlet lip,
	By her fine foot, straight leg and quivering thigh
	And the demesnes that there adjacent lie,
	That in thy likeness thou appear to us!
Benvolio:	And if he hear thee, thou wilt anger him.
Mercutio:	This cannot anger him. 'Twould anger him
	To raise a spirit in his mistress' circle
	Of some strange nature, letting it there stand
	Till she had laid it and conjured it down;
	That were some spite. My invocation
	Is fair and honest, in his mistress' name
	I conjure only but to raise up him.
Benvolio:	Come, he hath hid himself among these trees,
	To be consorted with the humorous night.
	Blind is his love and best befits the dark.
Mercutio:	If love be blind, love cannot hit the mark.

(Act 2, Scene 1, lines 7-33)

Q2 Read Act 3, Scene 5, lines 204-234. Explain the significance of the theme of religion in *Romeo and Juliet*. Use the extract to support your answer.

Q3 Read Act 5, Scene 3, lines 190-222. Explain how the feud between the Montague family and the Capulet family is presented in this extract and in the rest of the play.

Q4 Read Act 4, Scene 2, lines 16-47, then answer the questions below.

a) How is the relationship between Juliet and Capulet presented in this extract?

b) In this extract, Capulet is pleased that Juliet will marry Paris.
How does Shakespeare explore ideas about marriage in other parts of the play?
In your answer, you should consider:

- different ideas about marriage in the play
- how these ideas affect characters' actions in the play.

   Section Three — Context and Themes

Form and Structure of 'Romeo and Juliet'

Q1 In many tragedies, the hero's death is caused by their 'fatal flaw' — the main fault in their character. Do you think this is true of Romeo's death? Explain your answer.

....

....

....

Q2 Look at the stage directions from the start of Act 4, Scene 2 to line 16. What effect do they have on the scene's atmosphere? Explain your answer.

....

....

Q3 Fill in the gaps in the table below. The first one has been done for you.

Order of events in the play	The effect of ordering events in this way
a) The audience learns of Romeo's love for Rosaline before he meets Juliet.	It allows the audience to compare Romeo's love for Rosaline with his love for Juliet.
b) Capulet agrees to Paris and Juliet's engagement when Romeo is about to leave for Mantua.	
c) Juliet's body is discovered in her room, then Peter and the musicians trade humorous insults.	
d) Friar Lawrence finds out that his letter didn't get delivered after Romeo decides to kill himself.	

Q4 Read Act 2, Scene 3, lines 87-94. Explain how Friar Lawrence foreshadows Romeo's downfall in this passage of the play.

Foreshadowing is when a writer hints about something that will happen later in the text.

....

....

....

Q5 Act 3, Scene 4 is very short. Why do you think that Shakespeare uses a short scene at this point in the play?

....

....

....

Q6 Explain how each of the following events creates suspense for the audience.

a) At the start of the play, the Prince says that whoever next fights on Verona's streets because of the feud between the families will be executed. (Act 1, Scene 1)

....

....

b) Paris visits Juliet's tomb around the same time that Romeo is due to arrive there. (Act 5, Scene 3)

....

....

Q7 The fighting gets more and more violent as the play progresses. Why do you think Shakespeare might have structured the play in this way?

....

....

Q8 Which of the following do you think is the main 'turning point' in the fortunes of Romeo and Juliet: Mercutio's death or Juliet's decision to fake her own death? Explain your answer.

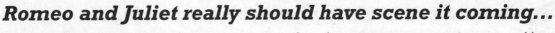

© Alastair Muir/REX/Shutterstock

....

....

....

....

PRACTICE TASK

Romeo and Juliet really should have scene it coming...

The stage directions say that Juliet appears at a window above Romeo in Act 2, Scene 2 and kneels down before Capulet in Act 3, Scene 5. Briefly explain the significance of each stage direction.

Mood and Atmosphere

Q1 What effect do the prologues have on the mood of the play? Support your answer with a quote.

....

....

....

....

Q2 Fill in the gaps in the table below. The first one has been done for you.

Setting	How the setting creates a certain atmosphere
a) Act 1, Scene 5: A party in the great hall of Capulet's mansion.	It is a busy occasion, which creates a lively atmosphere.
b) Act 2, Scene 6: Friar Lawrence's cell (a small, private room).	
c) Act 3, Scene 1: A hot day on Verona's streets.	

Q3 When the Nurse thinks that Juliet is dead in Act 4, Scene 5, she says that it is the "**Most lamentable day, most woeful day, / That ever, ever, I did yet behold!**" Explain what atmosphere is created by the language in this quote.

....

....

....

Q4 Briefly explain how the mood of the play changes when Mercutio dies.

....

....

Romeo is certainly prone to mood swings...

Read Act 2, Scene 4, lines 13-34. **How does Shakespeare create a light-hearted mood in this extract and at other points in the play?** Write an answer to this question, using quotes to back up your ideas.

Section Four — Shakespeare's Techniques

Dramatic Irony

Q1 Read Juliet's soliloquy at the start of Act 3, Scene 2.
How does dramatic irony create sympathy for Juliet in this passage?

Dramatic irony is when the audience knows something that the characters don't know.

....

....

Q2 Explain what effect dramatic irony has on the audience in each of the following scenes:

a) Romeo and Juliet don't know their families are enemies but the audience does. (Act 1, Scene 5)

....

....

b) Romeo thinks that Juliet is dead but the audience knows she's actually alive. (Act 5, Scene 1)

....

....

Q3 Read Act 5, Scene 3, lines 106-112. Romeo says he is going to die in order
to put a stop to his bad luck. Explain why this an example of dramatic irony.

....

....

....

© Bill Cooper/ArenaPAL

Q4 How does the way Shakespeare uses dramatic irony in Romeo and Juliet help to keep
the audience engaged? You should write about the play's events in your answer.

....

....

....

A love story, a few fight scenes — it's all very dramatic...

Romeo and Juliet is full of dramatic irony — examples include Romeo and Juliet's marriage and
Juliet's fake death, but the play is bursting with others. Be sure to explain their effects in the exam.

Poetry in Shakespeare

Q1 Find a quote that is written in blank verse.

Blank verse is a type of poetry. Its lines have 10 or 11 syllables, 5 main beats and they don't rhyme.

....

....

Q2 Romeo and Juliet's conversation in Act 1, Scene 5 is written in the form of a sonnet. What does this suggest about their feelings for each other?

A sonnet is a type of poem that has a strict rhyme scheme and is associated with romance.

....

....

Q3 Read Act 1, Scene 1, lines 66-74, then answer the following questions.

a) Shakespeare puts the phrase "A crutch, a crutch!" at the start of Lady Capulet's speech, rather than at the end. What effect does this have?

....

b) How does rhythm create a chaotic atmosphere in this passage?

....

....

Q4 Read Act 3, Scene 1, lines 126-136. Find a quote in the extract that includes a lot of short words. Then explain why you think Shakespeare uses so many short words in this passage.

Quote: ....

Explanation: ....

....

Q5 Why do you think Shakespeare gives Romeo a soliloquy just before his death?

....

....

We rehearsed the play in a car — it was poetry in motion...

A character's speech can sometimes be linked to their social class. Upper-class characters, such as the Prince, often use blank verse. Lower-class characters, like the Nurse, don't normally use a set rhythm.

Puns and Wordplay

Q1 Read the paragraph below and fill in the gaps using the words in the box.

A pun is sometimes formed when a word has more than one ....

or when two words are .... in the same way. Puns are usually

..............................., so Shakespeare often uses them to .... the audience.

> anger emotional entertain pronounced calm funny sad insult meaning

Q2 In Act 3, Scene 1, line 43, Mercutio uses a pun to twist
Tybalt's words. Explain why you think he does this.

....

....

....

....

© Geraint Lewis

Q3 In Act 3, Scene 5, Lady Capulet talks to Juliet about arranging to poison Romeo. Juliet
replies: "**if you could find out but a man / To bear a poison, I would temper it**" (lines 96-97).
"**Temper**" can mean 'mix' or 'weaken'. What is the effect of this pun? Explain your answer.

....

....

....

Q4 Romeo, Benvolio and Mercutio often use wordplay when speaking to one another.
What does their use of wordplay suggest about their relationship? Explain your answer.

....

....

....

PRACTICE TASK

Mercutio should be pun-ished for his terrible jokes...

Write down three examples of puns, each one from a different act of the play. For each one, write a
couple of sentences explaining how the pun is created and why Shakespeare might have included it.

Imagery and Symbolism

Q1 Read Act 1, Scene 4, lines 25-26. Describe how Romeo personifies love in these lines, then explain what this personification suggests about the nature of love.

....

....

....

Q2 In Act 1, Scene 3, lines 80-95, Lady Capulet uses an extended metaphor of a book to describe Paris. Explain why you think Shakespeare includes such a detailed metaphor in this passage.

....

....

....

Q3 Read Act 1, Scene 5, lines 92-109, then answer the following questions.

a) Find two examples of religious imagery in this passage.

Example 1: ....

Example 2: ....

b) What does the religious imagery in this extract suggest about Romeo and Juliet's relationship?

....

....

Q4 In Act 2, Scene 2, lines 80-84 and Act 5, Scene 3, lines 116-118, Romeo uses imagery to do with a 'pilot' (sailor). How and why does the way he uses this imagery change?

....

....

....

....

....

Section Four — Shakespeare's Techniques

Q5 The table below gives some examples of how light and darkness symbolise aspects of Romeo and Juliet's relationship. Fill in the gaps in the table. Some have been done for you.

Use of light and darkness	Quote	Effect
a) Romeo uses light imagery to describe Juliet.	**"she doth teach the torches to burn bright!"** (Act 1, Scene 5, line 43)	Comparing Juliet to a bright light shows how much her beauty makes her stand out to Romeo.
b) Juliet can't wait for darkness to come at night.		
c) Romeo and Juliet's deaths cause darkness.	**"A glooming peace this morning with it brings, / The sun, for sorrow, will not show his head."** (Act 5, Scene 3, lines 305-306)	

Q6 Read the following statements about the way natural imagery and symbolism are used in the play, then decide whether they are **true** or **false**.

                True   **False**

Shakespeare uses flower imagery to describe Romeo and Juliet's love. ☐ ☐

Nature always symbolises positive things in the play. ☐ ☐

The Nurse is the character who uses the most natural imagery. ☐ ☐

Juliet compares her love for Romeo to the sea in Act 2. ☐ ☐

Q7 How does imagery show Juliet's impatience with the Nurse in Act 2, Scene 5? Use a quote in your answer.

....

....

....

Q8 When Juliet's body is discovered in Act 4, Scene 5, Capulet compares her death to **"an untimely frost"**. How does this image reflect the way that time is presented in the play?

....

....

....

I bet Capulet's musicians love a bit of cymbal-ism...

It's a good idea to have plenty of examples of how Shakespeare uses imagery and symbolism stored in your brain — this will give you a chance to show off your language analysis skills in the exam.

 ☐   ☐   ☐

Working with Extracts

In the exam, there will be a question that asks you to write about an extract. Examiners love extract questions as they demonstrate your ability to discuss a short passage in detail. They're also a great opportunity for you to really focus on language analysis, showing that you understand how language creates meaning. This page will help you to develop the skills needed to ace any extract question.

Lady Capulet:	What say you? Can you love the gentleman?
	This night you shall behold him at our feast;
	Read o'er the volume of young Paris' face,
	And find delight writ there with beauty's pen.
	Examine every married lineament,
	And see how one another lends content
	And what obscured in this fair volume lies
	Find written in the margent of his eyes.
	This precious book of love, this unbound lover,
	To beautify him, only lacks a cover.
	The fish lives in the sea, and 'tis much pride
	For fair without the fair within to hide.
	That book in many's eyes doth share the glory,
	That in gold clasps locks in the golden story.
	So shall you share all that he doth possess,
	By having him, making yourself no less.
Nurse:	No less, nay, bigger. Women grow by men.
Lady Capulet:	Speak briefly, can you like of Paris' love?

(Act 1, Scene 3, lines 80-97)

Q1 Read through the extract above. Describe what has just happened in the play before this extract and what is about to happen after it.

....

....

Q2 Lady Capulet implies that Juliet could be Paris's "cover." What does this suggest?

....

Q3 In this extract, Lady Capulet uses rhyming couplets. What effect does this have?

....

....

Q4 In this passage, the Nurse refers to the sexual side of marriage. Find an example from elsewhere in the play when the Nurse talks about sexual love.

....

....

Section Four — Shakespeare's Techniques

Practice Questions

Now you're up to speed with Shakespeare's techniques, it's time to create your own masterpieces by taking on these practice exam questions. You'll need to write about Shakespeare's techniques in the exam, so try to include ideas about language, structure and form in these answers. If you get stuck, have a look back over your answers for this section. It's also a good idea to spend five minutes on a plan before you start writing.

Q1 How does Shakespeare create a tense atmosphere in *Romeo and Juliet*?
You must refer to the extract below and the play as a whole in your answer.

> **Juliet:** Farewell! God knows when we shall meet again.
> I have a faint cold fear thrills through my veins
> That almost freezes up the heat of life.
> I'll call them back again to comfort me.
> Nurse! What should she do here?
> My dismal scene I needs must act alone.
> Come, vial.
> What if this mixture do not work at all?
> Shall I be married then tomorrow morning?
> No, no, this shall forbid it; lie thou there.
>
> *Laying down her dagger*
>
> What if it be a poison which the Friar
> Subtly hath ministered to have me dead,
> Lest in this marriage he should be dishonoured,
> Because he married me before to Romeo?
> I fear it is, and yet methinks it should not,
> For he hath still been tried a holy man.
> How if, when I am laid into the tomb,
> I wake before the time that Romeo
> Come to redeem me? There's a fearful point!
> Shall I not then be stifled in the vault,
> To whose foul mouth no healthsome air breathes in,
> And there die strangled ere my Romeo comes?
>
> (Act 4, Scene 3, lines 14-35)

Q2 Read Act 5, Scene 1, lines 1-33. Write about how Shakespeare presents Romeo and Juliet's relationship as doomed. You should discuss the extract and the play as a whole.

Q3 Read Act 5, Scene 3, lines 1-21. Explain how Shakespeare presents the character of Paris in *Romeo and Juliet*. You should refer to the extract and the play as a whole.

Q4 Read Act 1, Scene 4, lines 11-43.

a) Explain what the extract shows the audience about the relationship between Romeo and Mercutio at this point in the play.

b) This scene takes place in a street. How are settings important to the play as a whole?

      Section Four — Shakespeare's Techniques

Understanding the Question

Underline key words in the question

Q1 Underline the most important words in the following questions.
The first one has been done for you.

a) <u>To what extent</u> is <u>Juliet</u> presented as a <u>good daughter</u> in the play?

b) Write about the significance of religion in *Romeo and Juliet*.

c) Explain how the relationship between Romeo and Mercutio is presented.

d) How does Shakespeare explore attitudes to marriage in *Romeo and Juliet*?

e) Write about the significance of Friar Lawrence in *Romeo and Juliet*.

f) How is the character of the Nurse presented in *Romeo and Juliet*?

g) Explain how the relationship between the Montague family and the Capulet family is presented.

Make sure you understand exam language

Q2 Match each exam question to the correct explanation of what you would
need to do to answer it. You'll only need to use each white box once.

a) To what extent is Juliet presented as a good daughter in the play?	**1)** Analyse how a theme contributes to the action of the play.
b) Write about the significance of religion in *Romeo and Juliet*.	**2)** Analyse how far a judgement or description is correct.
c) Explain how the relationship between Romeo and Mercutio is presented.	**3)** Analyse how Shakespeare presents different views about a theme in the play.
d) How does Shakespeare explore attitudes to marriage in *Romeo and Juliet*?	**4)** Analyse how a character contributes to the action and overall message of the play.
e) Write about the significance of Friar Lawrence in *Romeo and Juliet*.	**5)** Analyse how characters interact and impact on each other.

What sense through yonder question breaks?

When you're told to start your exam, it's hard not to just dive in and write as much as you can. But this won't
help you get a good grade — firstly, read the question several times and consider what it's really asking you.

Making a Rough Plan

Jot down your main ideas

Q1 Look at the exam question below, then complete the spider diagram with at least three more main points for answering it.

Don't forget to underline the key words in the question before you start.

Lady Capulet's language makes her sound distressed at losing her only daughter.

Read Act 4, Scene 5 from line 33 to line 64.
How is the theme of family presented in *Romeo and Juliet*?
Use the extract and the play as a whole in your answer.

Put your main points and examples in a logical order

Q2 Choose your three main points from Q1 and fill in the plan below, adding evidence (a quote or an example from the text) for each point.

One or two of your points should be about the extract from Q1.

(Introduction)

Point One: ....

Evidence: ....

Point Two: ....

Evidence: ....

Point Three: ....

Evidence: ....

(Conclusion)

A spider diagram? Well, the play is a tangled web of lies...

In the exam, it's really important that you make a plan before you start writing each answer. Plans help you to stay focused and help you to stick to the most relevant points. And they should only take around 5 minutes...

Making Links

Make links with other parts of the text

Q1 Look at the exam question and the table below. Complete the table with other relevant parts of the text which could be used to back up each point.

> How is the character of the Nurse presented in *Romeo and Juliet*?

Point	Example 1	Example 2
The Nurse is a comic character.	She interrupts Lady Capulet to tell the same story over and over again in Act 1, Scene 3.	
The Nurse is protective of Juliet.	She tries to stop Capulet from telling Juliet off in Act 3, Scene 5, arguing he shouldn't "rate her so".	
The Nurse is untrustworthy.	She deceives Capulet and Lady Capulet by keeping Juliet's marriage a secret.	

Extend your essay with other examples

You won't have time to do really detailed planning in the exam, so you should get into the habit of thinking of links when you're doing practice questions.

Q2 Take each of your points from the plan you made in Q2 on p.51, and write down another example from elsewhere in the text that you could include in your essay.

Example for Point One: ....

....

Example for Point Two: ....

....

Example for Point Three: ....

....

Make links, not war — pretty much the message of the play...

To show the examiner you have a solid understanding of the play, you have to be able to make links — this makes your answers more persuasive. Try noting down any links that you come across while reading the text.

Structuring Your Answer

P.E.E.D. stands for Point, Example, Explain, Develop

Q1 Read the following extract from an exam answer. Label each aspect of P.E.E.D.

> The feud between the families is shown to be extreme. In Act 3, Scene 1, Benvolio worries that the weather during "these hot days" will provoke a brawl. The idea that something as mundane as hot weather could spark violence between the families suggests that the feud has gone past reason. This shows that the feud is extreme to the point of being senseless. As a result, Romeo's and Juliet's deaths seem particularly unnecessary and tragic to the audience.

Embedding quotes is a great way to give evidence

Q2 Rewrite the following sentences so that a short part of the quote is embedded in each one.

a) Friar Lawrence thinks Romeo always has bad luck. — "And thou art wedded to calamity"

....

b) Juliet is distraught because of Romeo's banishment. — "Even so lies she, / Blubbering"

....

Structure your answer using the P.E.E.D. method

Q3 Use the P.E.E.D. method to structure a paragraph on your first point from Q2 on page 51.

Point: ....

....

Example: ....

....

Explain: ....

....

Develop: ....

....

[Insert obvious joke here]...

You should always use the P.E.E.D. structure in your exam as it helps to make your answers brilliantly clear and concise. A good way to remember the structure is to come up with a funny joke about it — the ruder the better.

Introductions and Conclusions

Give a clear answer to the question in your introduction

Q1 Read the introductions below, then decide which is better. Explain your choice.

> To what extent is Friar Lawrence presented as a responsible character in *Romeo and Juliet*?

a)
> In many ways, Friar Lawrence is presented by Shakespeare as a responsible character. This is shown by the way he tries to help Romeo and Juliet, and by his religious role as a Friar, which was a position of great responsibility in the 16th century. Despite this, some of his actions are also shown to be irresponsible and could be said to contribute to the play's tragic outcome.

b)
> Shakespeare presents Friar Lawrence as a caring character, who gives Romeo good advice. In this respect, he is like a father to Romeo. Friar Lawrence's status as a religious character also means that other characters consider him to be responsible. Religion is a particularly important theme in the play, as it has an impact on many of the main events and characters.

Better intro: .... Reason: ....

....

....

....

Don't write any new points in your conclusion

Q2 Read this conclusion to the exam question in Q1, then explain how it could be improved.

> In conclusion, Friar Lawrence is presented as irresponsible at times. He is therefore similar to the Nurse, who is helpful but also behaves irresponsibly. She allows Juliet to marry Romeo, despite knowing that he is a Montague, which means that her actions also lead to Romeo and Juliet's deaths.

....

....

....

....

My conclusion? Sending letters is a risky business...

Write an introduction and conclusion for the exam question on page 51. Make sure that you give a direct answer to the question in your introduction, and that the content you include in your conclusion is clear and relevant.

Writing about Context

Make sure you can link the play to its context

Q1 Match each statement with the relevant contextual information.

> **a)** Capulet becomes angry when Juliet refuses to marry his choice of husband.

> **1)** In the 16th century, marriage was an important way for girls to secure wealth and status.

> **b)** It often seems as though Juliet has a closer relationship with the Nurse than with her mother.

> **2)** 16th-century fathers were the head of the household and expected to be obeyed by their children.

> **c)** Lady Capulet is eager for Juliet to start thinking about marriage.

> **3)** Wealthy families in the 16th century often employed someone to raise their children.

Include context in your answer

Q2 Read the sample answer extract below and underline the contextual information.

> The character of Mercutio is used to create humour in the play. In Act 2, Scene 1, Mercutio jokingly refers to Romeo as a "poperin pear". This term is the name of a fruit, but is being used here as an innuendo to refer to genitals. In the 16th century, Shakespeare's plays were watched by people of all classes, so some audience members would have been illiterate. Including sexual innuendos was therefore an effective way for playwrights to entertain the whole audience at that time, as it meant audience members didn't have to rely on their knowledge of things like rare meanings of words.

Q3 Now write a paragraph on either your second or third point from page 51.
You should include contextual information and use the P.E.E.D. method.

....

....

....

....

....

....

Include some context or the examiner will be con-vexed...

In the exam, you need to show the examiner that you understand the relationship between the play and its context. There are loads of ways you can do this, just make sure your context is always relevant to the point you're making.

Linking Ideas and Paragraphs

Link your ideas so your argument is easy to follow

Q1   Rewrite the sample answer below so that the ideas are clearly linked.

> Shakespeare indicates that Romeo and Juliet's marriage is ill-fated. In Act 2, Scene 6, just before they get married, Friar Lawrence says that even the "sweetest honey" becomes "loathsome" when it's eaten in excess. Romeo and Juliet's happiness won't last. In Act 3, Scene 3, Friar Lawrence says Romeo is "wedded to calamity".

....

....

....

....

....

Q2   Write a paragraph using your remaining point from p.51. Make sure your ideas are properly linked.

....

....

....

....

....

Show how your paragraphs follow on from each other

Q3   Look at the paragraphs you have written on p.53, p.55 and on this page using your points from p.51. Write down linking words or phrases you could use to link them together in your answer.

Paragraphs to link	Linking word or phrase
Points 1 and 2	
Points 2 and 3	

Paragraphs should be like swords — a strong point is best...

Read the question carefully and make a plan before you write your answer. If you know what you want to argue before you start writing, then the links between your ideas will be a lot clearer. And remember to use P.E.E.D.

Marking Answer Extracts

Get familiar with the mark scheme

Grade band	An answer at this level...
8-9	• shows an insightful and critical personal response to the text • closely and perceptively analyses how the writer uses language, form and structure to create meaning and affect the reader, making use of highly relevant subject terminology • supports arguments with well-integrated, highly relevant and precise examples from the text • gives a detailed exploration of the relationship between the text and its context • uses highly varied vocabulary and sentence types, with mostly accurate spelling and punctuation
6-7	• shows a critical and observant personal response to the text • includes a thorough exploration of how the writer uses language, form and structure to create meaning and affect the reader, making use of appropriate subject terminology • supports arguments with integrated, well-chosen examples from the text • explores the relationship between the text and its context • uses a substantial range of vocabulary and sentence types, with generally accurate spelling and punctuation
4-5	• shows a thoughtful and clear personal response to the text • examines how the writer uses language, form and structure to create meaning and affect the reader, making some use of relevant subject terminology • integrates appropriate examples from the text • shows an understanding of contextual factors • uses a moderate range of vocabulary and sentence types, without spelling and punctuation errors which make the meaning unclear

Have a go at marking an answer extract

Q1 Using the mark scheme, put the sample answer extract below in a grade band and explain why.

> How is Tybalt presented as an aggressive character in *Romeo and Juliet*?

> Tybalt is shown to have an agressive personality. When Benvolio mentions peace, Tybalt tells him "I hate the word / As I hate hell". The fact that Tybalt dislikes peace suggests that he likes fighting, which is emphasised by the use of the strong verb "hate". Tybalt therefore has an aggressive personalty because he likes fighting. At the time Shakespeare was writing, many people in England believed that Italians were passionate.

Grade band: ....   Reason: ....

....

....

....

Marking Answer Extracts

Have a look at these extracts from answers to the question on p.57

Q1 For each extract, say what grade band you think it is in, then underline an example of where it meets each of the mark scheme criteria. Label each underlined point to show what it achieves.

a) Shakespeare presents Tybalt as aggressive through the contrast he forms with Romeo, who is portrayed as being more peaceful. In Act 1, Scene 5, despite Romeo's peaceable behaviour at Capulet's party, Tybalt vows that Romeo's intrusion will "convert to bitterest gall". Here, the repetition of sharp 't' sounds creates a harsh tone that makes Tybalt seem threatening. This contrasts with the language Romeo uses immediately afterwards, which is dominated by soft sibilant sounds. Romeo's gentle tone makes Tybalt's threatening language appear more extreme, highlighting Tybalt's aggressive nature to the audience. Tybalt's aggression is further emphasised through the contrast he forms with Romeo later in the play, when Tybalt reacts to Romeo's arrival in Act 3, Scene 1 by calling him "a villain", whereas Romeo reacts with "love".

In addition, Shakespeare presents Tybalt as aggressive through his willingness to kill others, which is emphasised by the structure of the play. In Act 1, Scene 5, Tybalt wants to fight Romeo despite Capulet's protests. By establishing this as a serious intention in the first act of the play, Shakespeare makes the later references to Tybalt's duel with Romeo seem more threatening, as the audience now knows not only that Tybalt is willing to pursue a fight but also that he is prepared to kill Romeo. Duels in the 16th century were rarely intended to kill people (they were normally used to wound someone in order to reclaim honour) so the fact that Romeo's life appears to be in danger emphasises Tybalt's aggression.

Grade band: ....

b) Shakespeare presents Tybalt as aggressive through the way he is viewed by other characters. For example, Benvolio emphasises Tybalt's role in the fighting in Act 3, Scene 1, calling him "deaf to peace". The word "deaf" means being unable to hear, which implies that Tybalt is unable to listen to any arguments for peace in the family feud. Benvolio's description therefore emphasises Tybalt's aggressive nature because it shows that there is no peaceful aspect to his character. However, Benvolio also exaggerates Tybalt's aggressive nature when he's talking to the Prince by leaving out the fact that it was Mercutio who provoked Tybalt. This means that Tybalt might not be as aggressive as other characters suggest, as the audience knows that Benvolio's description isn't fair.

Shakespeare also presents Tybalt as aggressive through the way he tries to provoke others. In Act 3, Scene 1, Tybalt twice refers to Romeo as "boy". This makes it seem like Tybalt is calling Romeo a child, which suggests he is trying to belittle Romeo in the hope of provoking him into fighting. This shows that Tybalt is an aggressive character because it suggests that he pursues opportunities for violence. In the 16th century, the word "boy" was also used to refer to servants. Social status was an important feature of 16th-century society, so suggesting that Romeo belongs to a lower class would have made Tybalt's comment seem insulting to an audience in Shakespeare's time. This may have made Tybalt seem even more aggressive to them.

Grade band: ....

Marking a Whole Answer

Now try marking this whole answer

Q1 Read the sample answer below. On page 60, put it in a grade band and explain your decision.

> Read Act 2, Scene 2, lines 52-78. Explore how Romeo and Juliet's love is presented in the play. You should write about the extract and the play as a whole in your answer.

If it helps you, label examples of where the answer meets the mark scheme criteria.

Shakespeare presents Romeo and Juliet's love as strong, but also as secretive, short-lived and ultimately doomed. The idea that their love is futile despite its strength suggests that it is not compatible with the demands of the society around them. It conflicts with ideas about loyalty and honour that result from the feud between the two families. The way that the lovers' tragic ends are made apparent to the audience from the start of the play also highlights the powerful role of fate in their relationship. Furthermore, Romeo and Juliet's love is presented as destructive, as its extreme nature contributes to their deaths.

In the extract, Romeo and Juliet's love is shown to be strong. When Juliet exclaims that the orchard walls are hard to climb, Romeo replies that "stony limits cannot hold love out". This metaphor suggests that their love cannot be impeded by obstacles, even when they are difficult or dangerous. The strength of their love is highlighted by the words "limits" and "hold". Both words relate to confinement and therefore stress the idea that their love is restricted, making Romeo's assertion that their love cannot be held back more meaningful. The power of their love is reinforced by the contrast it forms with Romeo's love for Rosaline, which follows the traditions of courtly love. The methodical way Romeo woos Rosaline seems artificial compared to the natural way that he and Juliet fall in love. This makes Romeo and Juliet's love seem true.

Even though their love is shown to be sincere, the extract suggests that secrecy is an integral part of Romeo and Juliet's love. Romeo uses "night's cloak" to "hide" him when he comes to declare his love for Juliet. The image of the cloak shows his fear of their love being uncovered and exposed to Capulet "eyes". The fact that this need for secrecy is acknowledged in the same scene that Romeo and Juliet reveal their feelings to each other indicates that it is a fundamental feature of their love. This is supported by the way that secrecy is linked to other important milestones of their love. For example, both their wedding and the consummation of their marriage take place off stage. This emphasises the private nature of their love, as the audience are deliberately distanced from the action.

Romeo and Juliet's love is also presented as dangerous. In the extract, Romeo tells Juliet that his name "is an enemy to thee", which shows that Romeo merely holding the name 'Montague' puts Juliet in danger. The internal rhyme of "enemy" and "thee" makes the words seem closely related, which suggests that the danger caused by Romeo's identity as a Montague is linked to the fact that Juliet is a Capulet. This implies that the feud is an unavoidable part of their love, suggesting that the danger posed to them by the feud will always be present. The ever-present sense of danger surrounding their love is reflected in Shakespeare's choice of setting. In 16th-century Britain, Italy was known as a place of conflict. For centuries, different areas had been ruled by different local governments. Struggles for power in these areas were common and political opposition could be punished by exile or death. This setting thus creates a violent backdrop for the couple's relationship, which makes the dangers associated with their love seem more credible.

Just as Romeo and Juliet are unable to escape the feud between their families, the tragic ending to their love is shown to be predetermined and therefore inescapable. In the Prologue to Act 1, Romeo and Juliet are described as "star-crossed lovers". Stars are

This answer continues on p.60. ➡

Marking a Whole Answer

associated with fate in the play, so the fact that Romeo and Juliet's relationship 'crosses' them implies their love goes against fate. The description therefore suggests that their love is doomed. This idea is furthered by the fact that the play contains elements of the tragic form, such as conflict, a flawed hero and repeated references to fate. As a tragedy's hero or heroine often dies, it's likely that the audience would expect the death of one or both of the title characters. This may have been especially relevant in Shakespeare's time, when the title of the play included the word 'tragedy'. As a result, from the start of the play the audience gets the impression that Romeo and Juliet's love is not only destined to be ill-fated, but also short-lived.

Shakespeare also uses the structure of the play to show that Romeo and Juliet's love is fleeting. In Act 2, Scene 2, Juliet tells Romeo that their love is too rash, but by the end of the scene asks him to arrange their marriage the very next day. This haste is reflected in the plot as a whole. Shakespeare arranges the action so that it spans five days, in which time Romeo and Juliet meet, marry and kill themselves. The speed of events creates a frantic atmosphere, as the audience gets the sense that Romeo and Juliet's love has become too serious too quickly, which makes it seem like events are speeding out of control. This frantic pace is added to by the performance time of the play. In the Prologue to Act 1, the Chorus references the fact that the play lasts only "two hours' traffic". The fact that the audience witnesses the whole of Romeo and Juliet's relationship in such a short amount of time makes their love seem even more short-lived.

Shakespeare presents Romeo and Juliet's love as destructive. In Act 3, Scene 2, when the Nurse informs Juliet that Romeo has been "banishèd", Juliet says that there is "no end" to "that word's death". This suggests that the word "banishèd" has a limitless power to 'kill', which implies that, for Juliet, being separated from Romeo is like a death sentence. Establishing death as the only alternative to their love highlights their love's destructive power. This is confirmed in Act 5, Scene 3, when both Romeo and Juliet kill themselves to escape living in a world without their love. This act would have seemed even more destructive to a 16th-century audience, who would have viewed suicide as a sin.

Romeo and Juliet's love is presented as resilient, despite the dangers and obstacles it faces, but it also appears to be powerless in preventing the tragic ending of the play. Their enduring love for each other becomes more important to them than staying alive, which ultimately leads to their deaths. In this way, their love is damaging and destructive.

Grade band: ....   Reasons: ....

....

....

....

....

....

Poor Mark — he's always being judged...

Knowing how to get a good mark in the exam is really important, so you should practise including things like language analysis, structure, form and context. That way, it'll be second nature by the time you're in the exam.

Writing Well

It might seem obvious, but it's important that you use the correct spelling, punctuation and grammar (SPaG for short) in your exam. 5% of the marks in your English Literature GCSE are for writing well, which includes using a wide range of vocabulary, technical terms and sentence structures, as well as accurate SPaG. It's best if you leave yourself a few minutes at the end of the exam to check over your work and correct any mistakes. If you see one, draw a line through it and put your correction above.

Q1 Read the sample answer below. Underline all of the SPaG mistakes, then correct them. One has already been done for you.

> an
> Friar Lawrence is a important figure because his actions affect the plot. For instants, he
>
> helps Romeo and Juliet to get married and gave Juliet the drug that makes her appear dead.
>
> Dispite his good intentions, these actions contribute to the plays tragic ending. This makes
>
> it unclear whether Shakespeare wants the audience to see him as helpful or irresponsable.

Q2 Match each technical term to the correct example.
You'll only need to use each example once.

a) Metaphor	**1)** "For never was a story of more woe / Than this of Juliet and her Romeo"
b) Simile	**2)** "Arise, fair sun, and kill the envious moon"
c) Rhyming couplet	**3)** "O brawling love, O loving hate"
d) Oxymoron	**4)** "It is too rash, too unadvised, too sudden, / Too like the lightning"
e) Pun	**5)** "Love is a smoke raised with the fume of sighs"
f) Personification	**6)** "You have dancing shoes / With nimble soles, I have a soul of lead"

Practice Questions

It's time to put what you've learned about writing a great essay into action. Answer each of the questions on this page under exam conditions — spend 5 minutes writing a plan, then 40 minutes on the answer.

Q1 Read the extract below from Act 2, Scene 2, then answer the following questions.

a) Explain what the extract shows to the audience about Juliet's state of mind at this point in the play. Refer only to the extract in your answer.

> **Juliet:** O Romeo, Romeo, wherefore art thou Romeo?
> Deny thy father and refuse thy name.
> Or if thou wilt not, be but sworn my love,
> And I'll no longer be a Capulet.
>
> **Romeo:** (*Aside*) Shall I hear more, or shall I speak at this?
>
> **Juliet:** 'Tis but thy name that is my enemy —
> Thou art thyself, though not a Montague.
> What's Montague? It is nor hand nor foot,
> Nor arm nor face, nor any other part
> Belonging to a man. O be some other name!
> What's in a name? That which we call a rose
> By any other word would smell as sweet;
> So Romeo would, were he not Romeo called,
> Retain that dear perfection which he owes
> Without that title. Romeo, doff thy name,
> And for thy name, which is no part of thee,
> Take all myself.
>
> (Act 2, Scene 2, lines 33-49)

b) 'Although there are only three fight scenes in the play, violence is important in *Romeo and Juliet*.' Explain how violence is important to the play.

Q2 Read Act 2, Scene 3, lines 65-94. How is Romeo presented as immature in the play? Refer to the extract and to the play as a whole.

Q3 Read Act 3, Scene 1, lines 138-171. Explain how Shakespeare presents Benvolio in this extract and in the rest of the play.

Q4 Read Act 5, Scene 3, lines 151-170.

a) Explain how Juliet is presented as a determined character in this extract.

b) In this extract, Juliet kills herself, which was considered a sin in the 16th century. Explain the significance of sin in other parts of the play. You should consider:
- where ideas about sin appear in the play
- how sins influence events in the play.

Answers

Section One — Analysis of Acts

Page 2: Act One — Prologue and Scene 1

1. The feud between the Montague and Capulet families.
2. 'Star-crossed' means 'unlucky', so the fact that Romeo and Juliet are "star-crossed lovers" means that their relationship is doomed.
3. He deliberately insults them by biting his thumb.
4. true, false, false, false, true
5. E.g. He feels unhappy because he's in love with someone who won't love him in return. He feels confused about how he can be in love and unhappy at the same time.
6. Because she has decided to remain a virgin.

Page 3: Act One — Scenes 2 and 3

1. a) E.g. "My child is yet a stranger in the world". (line 8)
   b) E.g. "woo her, gentle Paris, get her heart". (line 16)
2. Benvolio wants to show Romeo other girls, to prove that Rosaline isn't the only one for him. Romeo wants to go because he'll see Rosaline there.
3. E.g. They get the impression that she is rude and unrefined because she makes comments and jokes about sex. She also seems caring towards Juliet, who she treats like a daughter.
4. E.g. She thinks he has lots of good qualities. She says he is handsome and thinks he is kind-hearted.
5. She agrees to "look" at Paris and she says that she'll behave in a way that Lady Capulet would approve of.

Page 4: Act One — Scenes 4 and 5

1. E.g. It suggests that he is intelligent and funny because he makes clever puns. It also suggests that he is rude, as he makes several jokes about sex.
2. E.g. He fears it will lead to something bad happening.
3. The statements should be numbered 2, 4, 6, 3, 1, 5.
4. E.g. He doesn't want him to cause a disturbance. / Romeo isn't behaving in a disrespectful manner.
5. E.g. Romeo, her true love, is a member of the Montague family, which is her family's sworn enemy.
Task: Here are some points you could have included:
   - Juliet: She is in love with Romeo but feels conflicted because he is a Montague.
   - Benvolio: He is concerned about Romeo because he is so miserable about Rosaline, and wants to make him feel happier.
   - Mercutio: He is frustrated that Romeo is miserable and finds his obsession with love funny.
   - Tybalt: He is angry with Romeo because he thinks Romeo insulted his family's honour by attending the Capulet party.

Page 5: Act Two — Prologue, Scene 1 and Scene 2

1. E.g. It says that Juliet is Romeo's "foe supposed", which highlights that they will be in danger if their love is discovered.
2. E.g. To provoke Romeo into coming out of hiding. He thinks that being rude about Rosaline will make Romeo so angry that he'll want to confront Mercutio.
3. E.g. Because Romeo's identity as a Montague is the main reason that her relationship with him would be forbidden.
4. a) E.g. "If they do see thee, they will murder thee." (line 70)
   b) E.g. "would a maiden blush bepaint my cheek / For that which thou hast heard me speak tonight." (lines 86-87)
5. E.g. They emphasise to the audience that Romeo and Juliet's relationship is restricted, as they show Juliet is repeatedly interrupted and called away from Romeo.

Page 6: Act Two — Scenes 3 and 4

1. E.g. Romeo and Friar Lawrence appear to have a close relationship. Friar Lawrence is affectionate towards Romeo, calling him "my good son". Romeo also appears to confide in Friar Lawrence, as he tells him about his love for Juliet.
2. E.g. He has seen how quickly Romeo has fallen out of love with Rosaline, so he doubts that Romeo is really in love with Juliet.
3. Tybalt has challenged Romeo to a duel.
4. E.g. In Act 1 Scene 4, he dismisses Mercutio's jokes, whereas in this passage he joins in with Mercutio by making lots of jokes

and puns himself.
5. E.g. She thinks it's the right thing to do. She calls Romeo's proposal a "gentlemanlike offer" and agrees to help them.

Page 7: Act Two — Scenes 5 and 6

1. a) E.g. "speak, good, good Nurse, speak." (line 28)
   b) E.g. "Beshrew your heart for sending me about, / To catch my death". (lines 51-52)
2. E.g. Juliet must go to Friar Lawrence's cell, pretending to make a confession. There she will marry Romeo. That night, Romeo will climb to her bedroom using a ladder fetched for him by the Nurse.
3. E.g. "These violent delights" refers to the strength and passion of Romeo and Juliet's love, so the quote implies that their relationship will have a "violent" end.
4. E.g. So the Capulets don't wonder why Juliet is taking so long. / He doesn't want to get caught while performing the wedding.
5. E.g. It makes the wedding seemed rushed and secretive.
Task: Here are some points you could have included:
   - The play is set in Verona in Italy, where a fight breaks out between two feuding families: the Montagues and the Capulets.
   - The Montagues' son, Romeo, is in love with Rosaline, who does not love him back. Romeo's cousin, Benvolio, suggests they go to Capulet's party to help Romeo forget about Rosaline.
   - Meanwhile, Paris, a count, wants to marry Juliet and plans to woo her at Capulet's party.
   - However, after arriving at the party, Romeo and Juliet fall in love, only to find out they are from their enemies' households.
   - After the party, Romeo sneaks into the Capulets' orchard and speaks to Juliet while she is standing at her window. They decide to get married.
   - With the help of Friar Lawrence and Juliet's nurse, Romeo organises the wedding. Romeo and Juliet marry that afternoon.

Page 8: Act Three — Scene 1

1. E.g. To create a sense of danger. The fact that the atmosphere is tense makes conflict seem more likely.
2. The statements should be numbered 4, 3, 1, 5, 2.
3. E.g. He doesn't want to harm Tybalt as they are now related. / The Prince has banned them from fighting in the streets.
4. a) Mercutio — The Montague and Capulet families should be cursed for the trouble caused by their continued feud.
   b) Romeo — Romeo's actions are being driven by his anger at Mercutio's death.
5. E.g. He understands that Romeo only killed Tybalt because Tybalt had killed Romeo's friend, Mercutio.

Page 9: Act Three — Scenes 2 and 3

1. a) E.g. "For who is living, if those two are gone?" (line 68)
   b) E.g. "Alack the day, he's gone, he's killed, he's dead!" (line 39)
2. E.g. Juliet uses contradictory phrases, which show that her feelings are conflicted. She finds it hard to accept that the person she loves is capable of her cousin's murder.
3. E.g. She scolds herself for "talking ill" of Romeo and says that her distress at his banishment is greater than the death of "ten thousand Tybalts."
4. E.g. He feels distraught and agitated at the idea of being separated from Juliet.
5. E.g. He suggests that Romeo should be grateful because he wasn't killed by Tybalt, he has been exiled rather than executed, and Juliet is alive.
6. E.g. He is excited that he can go to Juliet on their wedding night.

Page 10: Act Three — Scenes 4 and 5

1. E.g. "she will be ruled / In all respects by me". (lines 13-14)
2. E.g. Having a big celebration so soon after Tybalt's death might be disrespectful.
3. a) False: E.g. "It was the nightingale, and not the lark". (line 2)
   b) True: E.g. "Evermore weeping for your cousin's death?" (line 69)
   c) True: E.g. "now I'll tell thee joyful tidings". (line 104)
4. E.g. Capulet insults Juliet, calling her a "disobedient wretch". His brutal reaction seems unfair, especially as Juliet begs him to listen to her. This makes him seem cruel.

Answers

5.   E.g. Because the Nurse initially encouraged her to marry Romeo. She feels abandoned by the person she confided in.

Task: Here are some points you could have included:
   • Family honour is important to the Montague and Capulet families. Romeo attended Capulet's party, which led to Tybalt feeling that his family's honour had been disgraced. He challenged Romeo to a duel, which he hoped to fight when he met Mercutio and Benvolio.
   • Romeo's marriage to Juliet meant he would not fight Tybalt himself, because it would mean fighting his wife's cousin, which led to Mercutio fighting in his place.
   • Mercutio was skilled in using puns and wordplay to mock people. This allowed him to provoke Tybalt into fighting him instead of Romeo.

Page 11: Act Four — Scenes 1, 2 and 3

1.   E.g. She is polite but not friendly. Her statement "What must be shall be" shows Paris no warmth or enthusiasm.
2.   E.g. He feels responsible for her as he married her to Romeo. He also knows she will be committing a sin if she marries Paris.
3.   E.g. He believes she should be obedient towards him.
4.   E.g. He wants it to take place before Juliet has a chance to change her mind again.
5.   E.g. She asks Lady Capulet to let the Nurse help with the preparations for the wedding.
6.   E.g. The gruesome imagery in the passage makes the idea of waking up in the tomb terrifying. The fact that Juliet is still willing to go through with the plan shows her determination.

Page 12: Act Four — Scenes 4 and 5

1.   E.g. They joke with the guests and with each other.
2.   They know that the Nurse will soon discover Juliet's body, as they witnessed Juliet taking the potion in the previous scene.
3.   E.g. She curses the day she was born, which shows that she is distressed.
4.   E.g. He believes his only daughter has died before marrying, so there is nobody to continue the family line.
5.   E.g. The audience becomes more sympathetic towards Lady Capulet. She calls Juliet's death the "most miserable hour", which shows that she genuinely loved her.
6.   E.g. He wants to get Juliet's body into the tomb as quickly as possible, in case she wakes up beforehand.

Task: Your letter should have covered the following points:
   • Juliet is to be married to Paris.
   • Friar Lawrence has given her a potion which she will drink.
   • The potion will put her to sleep and make it look like she has died.
   • Romeo should go to the Capulet tomb and be there when Juliet wakes up.
   • Romeo and Juliet will then travel to Mantua that night.

Page 13: Act Five — Scenes 1 and 2

1.   E.g. In his dream Juliet finds him dead, which is unsettling because the audience knows he'll die before the end of the play.
2.   E.g. No, because he is acting on the account of one person. If he waits he might hear from someone else in Verona, like Friar Lawrence. **Or** e.g. Yes. It's likely the news is true, because Balthasar has not received a letter to give to Romeo from Friar Lawrence.
3.   E.g. "Famine is in thy cheek". (line 69)
4.   E.g. He tells the apothecary to ignore the fact that selling him poison is illegal, because the law hasn't been good to him.
5.   The guards prevented him from travelling because they were scared he might have been infected by disease.
6.   Send another letter to Romeo. / Go to the tomb to be there when Juliet wakes up.

Page 14: Act Five — Scene 3

1.   flowers, Balthasar, Montague, arresting
2.   E.g. "Sweet flower, with flowers thy bridal bed I strew". (line 12)
3.   He identifies Romeo as the Montague who killed Tybalt. He

assumes Romeo wants to take further revenge on Tybalt and the Capulets.
4.   E.g. Quote: "tempt not a desperate man." (line 59)
        Explanation: He is pleading with Paris not to provoke him, which suggests that he wants to avoid a fight.
5.   E.g. The audience know that Juliet is alive. They hope Juliet will wake up before Romeo dies, which increases the tension as they watch Romeo kill himself.

Page 15: Act Five — Scene 3 continued

1.   You should have ticked the first and third statements.
2.   E.g. In order to make the audience compare Romeo's dream (where Juliet brings him back from the dead) and this scene. It provides hope for the audience that Romeo will wake up.
3.   The statements should be numbered 3, 1, 6, 4, 5, 2.
4.   E.g. Friar Lawrence's speech accurately describes the events that led to Romeo's and Juliet's deaths. This suggests he is honest as he does not try to hide any of the details, including his own involvement.
5.   E.g. The Montagues and Capulets decide to end the feud.

Task: Here are some points you could have included:
   • Sunday: There is a street fight in Verona, after which the Prince says all Montagues and Capulets who fight again will be executed. / A party takes place at Capulet's house, at which Romeo and Juliet meet for the first time. / Juliet speaks to Romeo from her window and they decide to get married.
   • Monday: Romeo makes the wedding plans. / Romeo and Juliet are married. / Mercutio and Tybalt are killed. / Romeo is banished. / Romeo hides at Friar Lawrence's cell, then goes to see Juliet in her room for their wedding night. / Capulet says Paris can marry Juliet.
   • Tuesday: Romeo leaves Juliet's bedroom. / Juliet hears about her wedding to Paris and goes to see Friar Lawrence. / Juliet takes the sleeping potion.
   • Wednesday: The Nurse finds Juliet's apparently dead body. / Romeo hears that Juliet is dead and buys poison.
   • Wednesday night / Thursday morning: Paris and Romeo fight at the Capulet tomb. / Romeo kills himself. / Juliet kills herself. / Montague and Capulet agree to end the feud.

Page 16: Using Quotes

1.   true, true, false, false, false
2. b) E.g. The fact that Romeo calls Juliet a "bright angel" suggests he thinks she's radiant.
    c) E.g. In Act One, the Prince thinks that the people who started the fight are "vile".
    d) E.g. Paris explains that the "inundation" of Juliet's tears caused Capulet to move the marriage forward to comfort her.
    e) E.g. Romeo can't see any sign of "death's pale flag" in Juliet's face.

Page 17: P.E.E.D.

1. a) Explain
    b) Develop
2. a) E.g. This suggests that Romeo was infatuated with Rosaline, but did not love her.
    b) E.g. Mercutio talks about Romeo raising "a spirit in his mistress' circle".

Section Two — Characters

Pages 18-19: Romeo

1. b) E.g. Romeo can be irrational when he's in love.
    c) E.g. Romeo was never in love with Rosaline / Romeo falls in and out of love easily.
    d) E.g. Romeo is passionate and impulsive.
    e) E.g. Romeo can be sociable and witty.
2.   E.g. At the start of the play, Romeo associates love with misery. When he's in love with Juliet, he associates it with happiness. He says that no sorrow can counter the "exchange of joy" he feels in her presence.

Answers

3. E.g. "is not this better now than groaning for love?"
(Act 2, Scene 4, line 78)
4. E.g. Meaning: You're disgracing your looks, your love and your intelligence.
Explanation: It suggests that Romeo's behaviour is irrational, as he's not thinking clearly and isn't appreciating what he still has.
5. a) E.g. "O brawling love, O loving hate".
(Act 1, Scene 1, line 170)
b) E.g. "let us hence — I stand on sudden haste."
(Act 2, Scene 3, line 93)
c) E.g. "Nurse, commend me to thy lady and mistress."
(Act 2, Scene 4, line 152)
6. E.g. To show that Romeo is more interested in love than in the feud. It makes his murder of Tybalt more shocking and shows he can't escape the feud.
7. E.g. Yes, because the fact that he loves Juliet means that he's now afraid of fighting Tybalt. He worries about hurting him now that they are related. He might also be scared that fighting him would upset Juliet. **Or** e.g. No, because he decides to stop the fighting. This is arguably braver than duelling with Tybalt because it shows that Romeo is willing to sacrifice his family's honour for his love for Juliet.
8. Romeo is initially in good spirits, but appears "pale and wild" to Balthasar after hearing about Juliet's supposed death. Despite this, he is calm and determined, giving orders like "get me ink and paper." This might show that he is in shock.
Exam Practice:
Your answer should have an introduction, several paragraphs developing different ideas and a conclusion. You may have covered some of the following points:
• Romeo is presented as passionate in his grief in this extract. In Act 3, Scene 3, Romeo's anger at himself for murdering Tybalt makes him seem like "an ill-beseeming beast". The word 'beast' suggests an untamed animal, which indicates that Romeo's emotions are raw and uncivilised. The idea that Romeo's passionate sadness makes him wild is emphasised in the stage directions, which state that Romeo takes out his dagger. This suggests he is considering suicide, which would have made him seem particularly desperate to a 16th-century audience, as they would have seen suicide as a crime.
• Romeo is presented as passionate in his love for Juliet. In Act 2, Scene 2, Romeo uses religious imagery to describe her, calling her a "bright angel" and saying that she is "o'er my head". The comparison of Juliet to an angel suggests that she is a pure, perfect being, while the way he positions her above him suggests that his passion leads him to worship her. Worshipping anyone other than God was considered a sin in the 16th century, so this would have highlighted the extreme nature of Romeo's passion for Juliet to the audience.
• Romeo is presented as passionate in his loyalty to Mercutio. In Act 3, Scene 1, Romeo's efforts to remain peaceful are undermined by his "fire-eyed fury" when his friend is killed. The idea that Romeo has fire in his eyes suggests that his anger is so intense, he is burning inside and giving off heat. This image implies that Romeo's fury at Mercutio's murder consumes him, which highlights the deep-rooted and heart-felt nature of his loyalty. Passion and loyalty are linked from the start of the play, when the Montague and Capulet servants cannot ignore each others' insults because of their fierce sense of family honour.

Pages 20-21: Juliet

1. a) E.g. "Thy purpose marriage, send me word tomorrow".
(Act 2, Scene 2, line 144)
b) E.g. "I'll to the Friar to know his remedy".
(Act 3, Scene 5, line 241)
c) E.g. "bring in cloudy night immediately."
(Act 3, Scene 2, line 4)
2. E.g. It suggests that Juliet has a realistic view of love. She is aware that the passion and true love are different things, and believes that true love lasts longer than passion.
3. E.g. She uses gruesome language to describe the things she would do to avoid marrying Paris, like "hide" with "yellow

chapless skulls". This shows how strongly she opposes the idea.
4. E.g. Brave, because if the plan worked and she moved to Mantua, she'd never be able to return to Verona, so she'd never see her family again. **Or** e.g. Foolish, because she blindly trusts Friar Lawrence to carry out the plan while she is in the tomb, even though he acted recklessly in marrying her to Romeo in the first place.
5. E.g. By Act 3, Scene 5, Juliet has decided to prioritise her love for Romeo over her love for her family. She has given her family name away by getting married and remains loyal to Romeo, even though he has killed her cousin, Tybalt.
6. false, false, true, false
7. E.g. It emphasises how quickly she loses her innocence. Even though she is only 13, she soon has to deal with very adult situations. By the end of the play she has had a secret marriage, lost her virginity and killed herself.
8. E.g. Yes, because it shows she is loyal to her husband, Romeo, despite the pressures she faces from her family. She is also standing by the principles of her religion, which state that being married to two people at once is a sin. **Or** e.g. No, because it shows she is willing to disrespect her parents by refusing to marry their chosen suitor. It also shows she is disloyal to her family, because she chooses to remain loyal to their enemy's son.

Page 22: Mercutio

1. E.g. He is less serious. / He is less polite.
2. a) E.g. "what saucy merchant was this".
(Act 2, Scene 4, lines 127-128)
b) E.g. "A gentleman, Nurse, that loves to hear himself talk".
(Act 2, Scene 4, line 129)
c) E.g. "brave Mercutio is dead." (Act 3, Scene 1, line 112)
3. E.g. Romeo's love for Mercutio causes him to kill Tybalt, which is an important turning point in the action of the play.
4. E.g. The way Mercutio outspokenly mocks others helps to provoke Tybalt into fighting. He insults Tybalt's honour by saying he will "dry-beat" him. His confrontational attitude also helps to escalate the feud, as his death sparks further conflict.

Page 23: Tybalt & Benvolio

1. E.g. "Put up your swords". (Act 1, Scene 1, line 58) / "I do but keep the peace." (Act 1, Scene 1, line 61)
2. a) E.g. He demands to fight Romeo at Capulet's party.
b) E.g. He is told not to fight Romeo at the party, but still challenges him to a duel.
3. E.g. He doesn't mention that Mercutio started the fight by provoking Tybalt. This suggests he is a loyal friend. It also suggests he isn't completely trustworthy, because he's not telling the full truth to the Prince.
4. E.g. That there is another side to the character they see on the stage. It shows he can be friendly with people who aren't Montagues.
Task: Here are some points you could have included about Tybalt:
• He is quick and nimble like a cat. Mercutio says that he "keeps time, distance, and proportion" when he fights.
• Ceremony is important to him, just as it would be to a Prince. Mercutio calls him a "courageous captain of compliments". When Shakespeare was writing, 'compliment' was another word for 'etiquette'. This suggests Tybalt focuses on the formal, ceremonial aspects of duelling.
Here are some points you could have included about Benvolio:
• He appears to seek peace over conflict, saying he's trying to "keep the peace" at the start of the play.
• He shows compassion towards Montague and Lady Montague in Act 1, Scene 1. He tries to find out what's wrong with Romeo on their behalf as he knows they're worried about him.

Page 24: The Montagues

1. E.g. Montague: He is irritable.
Lady Montague: She is peaceful.
2. a) E.g. "Black and portentous must this humour prove".
(Act 1, Scene 1, line 135)

Answers

b) E.g. "I neither know it, nor can learn of him."
(Act 1, Scene 1, line 138)

3. E.g. She dies as a result of her grief for Romeo's banishment, which suggests she is caring, as the idea of being parted from Romeo is too much for her to bear.

4. E.g. After Romeo and Juliet die, he takes responsibility for his role in their deaths. He doesn't do this after Mercutio and Tybalt's deaths, instead trying to ensure that his family avoids blame by arguing that Romeo only did "what the law should".

Task: If you answered 'yes', here are some points you could have included:
- Montague and Lady Montague seem less impulsive than Capulet and Lady Capulet. For example, in Act 3, Scene 1, Lady Capulet and Montague react differently to the fight between Tybalt and Romeo. Lady Capulet demands that Romeo is executed, whereas Montague reasons using the law. He therefore seems more capable of controlling his emotions.
- Shakespeare suggests that Lady Montague opposes the feud more than Lady Capulet. In Act 1, Scene 1, Lady Montague tells Montague that he shouldn't move "one foot to seek a foe". On the other hand, when Capulet tells his wife that Montague "is come", she doesn't try to intervene.

If you answered 'no', here are some points you could have included:
- Although Lady Montague tries to keep the peace in Act 1, Scene 1, Montague appears as happy to fight as Capulet does. This shows that they are both responsible.
- Capulet is the first to seek to end the feud after Romeo and Juliet's deaths, not Montague. His readiness to end the feud may suggest he is quicker to understand the destructive effects of the feud than Montague.

Page 25: The Capulets

1. b) E.g. She approves of Paris as a suitor.
   c) E.g. She cares about Juliet.

2. E.g. To make his response to Juliet's refusal to marry Paris in Act 3, Scene 5 more shocking.

3. E.g. It shows she is quite cold-hearted because she is unsympathetic towards Juliet and focuses on punishing Romeo instead.

4. E.g. "Come, stir, stir, stir!" (Act 4, Scene 4, line 3)

5. E.g. He repeats words and uses a lot of rhetorical questions, like "How, will she none?", which suggests he is shocked by her refusal to comply with his wishes.

Page 26: Nurse

1. E.g. "Lord, Lord! When 'twas a little prating thing" (Act 2, Scene 4, lines 178-179) / "I'll find Romeo / To comfort you" (Act 3, Scene 2, lines 138-139)

2. E.g. It suggests the Nurse enjoys teasing Juliet and that she has a rude sense of humour.

3. E.g. She acts as a messenger between Romeo and Juliet. Juliet has limited freedom to leave the house, so the Nurse helps her and Romeo to communicate when they are apart.

4. E.g. The Nurse's change of heart about Paris alters her relationship with Juliet. From this point in the play, the Nurse is no longer included in Juliet's plans and has lost Juliet's trust.

5. E.g. Yes, because she deceived Capulet and Lady Capulet and put Juliet in danger. **Or** e.g. No, because it was the feud that killed Juliet rather than her marriage to Romeo, which the Nurse helped to organise out of love for Juliet.

Page 27: Friar Lawrence

1. E.g. He cares deeply about Verona and wants to help everyone by putting the feud to an end. / He is calculating and is happy to take advantage of the love of a young couple for his own purposes.

2. E.g. "the sweetest honey / Is loathsome in his own deliciousness". (Act 2, Scene 6, lines 11-12) / "These violent delights have violent ends". (Act 2, Scene 6, line 9)

3. E.g. Friar Lawrence marries Romeo and Juliet in haste, without thinking properly about the consequences. As a result, he is

obliged to help them when things go wrong and eventually plays a part in their deaths.

4. E.g. In Act 5, he runs away when he hears the watchmen coming.

5. E.g. The Nurse says she could stay at Friar Lawrence's cell "all the night / To hear good counsel." The fact that the Nurse would be willing to stay all night to listen to the Friar emphasises how much she trusts and respects his opinion.

Task: Here are some points you could have included:
- He is irresponsible. He has doubts about Romeo and Juliet's love but decides to marry them anyway. His plan to reunite Romeo and Juliet is very dangerous, particularly for Juliet.
- He is calculating. He marries Romeo and Juliet in the hope that their marriage will lead to an end to the feud, despite the potential dangers for the couple.
- He is deceitful. He lies to the Nurse, Lady Capulet, Capulet and Paris by pretending that Juliet is dead, when in fact she's just asleep.

Page 28: Paris, Prince & Others

1. a) E.g. "Younger than she are happy mothers made."
   (Act 1, Scene 2, line 12)
   b) E.g. "Madam, good night. Commend me to your daughter."
   (Act 3, Scene 4, line 9)

2. E.g. Kindly, because he greets her with affection when she arrives, and reacts patiently when she replies sharply to his remarks. **Or** e.g. Arrogantly, because he refers to her as his wife when they haven't married yet. He also assumes that she's in love with him, telling her not to "deny" that she loves him.

3. E.g. He uses imperatives, for example "hear the sentence of your movèd Prince." This shows his authority because he expects others to do as he says. He also uses disrespectful language, for example in Act 1, Scene 1, he calls the brawlers "beasts". The fact that he can insult them shows the power he has over them.

4. E.g. Balthasar, because he has a bigger role than Peter. He brings Romeo false news of Juliet's death and is present when Romeo goes into the tomb in Act 5. **Or** e.g. Peter, because he's a greater source of comedy in the play. He uses wordplay to mock the Nurse in Act 2, Scene 4 and provides comic relief after Juliet's 'death'. This comedy keeps the audience entertained.

Page 29: Making Links

1. You could have used the following examples:
   Romeo — He writes poetry to Rosaline. / He falls in love with Juliet at first sight.
   Juliet — She kisses Romeo the first time she meets him. / She agrees to marry Romeo the day she meets him.
   Nurse — She refers to Juliet as a "lamb". / She claims that Juliet was the "prettiest babe that e'er I nurs'd."

2. You could have made the following points:
   Mercutio — He is unromantic, e.g. In Act 2, Scene 1, he mocks Romeo's sentimental view of love. / He uses lots of sexual puns.
   Tybalt — He is violent, e.g. He threatens to start a sword fight with Romeo at the party. / He kills Mercutio.
   Benvolio — He tries to maintain peace between the families, e.g. He tries to stop the fight at the start of the play. / He helps to convince the Prince to banish Romeo rather than kill him for murdering Tybalt.

Page 30: Practice Questions

Your answers should have an introduction, several paragraphs developing different ideas and a conclusion. You may have covered some of the following points:

1. - Shakespeare presents the Nurse as responsible, as she always tries to do what she thinks is best for Juliet. In this extract, the Nurse warns Romeo not to lead Juliet into a "fool's paradise" and take advantage of her. Later in the play, the Nurse goes to find Romeo "To comfort" Juliet. These actions show that she is consistently committed to Juliet, which suggests that she can be trusted to look after her interests. The Nurse's responsible nature is also highlighted by the fact that she acts as a maternal figure to Juliet. As a nurse, she has raised and cared for Juliet since she was a baby.

Answers

- Shakespeare presents the Nurse as irresponsible because she is absent-minded. This is reflected in her language. At the start of the extract, the majority of the Nurse's dialogue is made up of one long sentence, in which the frequent commas and semi-colons create an irregular rhythm. This makes her speech seem long and rambling, which suggests that she is inattentive and easily distracted. Even though she has little time to deliver Juliet's message, she is immediately diverted from her task, which shows that she is unreliable. Shakespeare may have made the Nurse irresponsible and easily distracted for comedic effect. He often used servants in this way in his other plays.
- Elsewhere in the play, Shakespeare presents the Nurse as irresponsible because she keeps secrets about Juliet from her employers. In Act 2, Scene 5, the Nurse deceives Capulet and Lady Capulet by planning to allow Romeo to spend the night with Juliet without their knowledge. In the 16th century, girls from noble families were not usually allowed to spend time in the company of suitors without supervision, so the audience would have considered the Nurse's deception to be irresponsible. The Nurse's deception of Capulet and Lady Capulet continues throughout the play, which suggests that it is in her nature to be irresponsible.

2. a)
- In the extract, Shakespeare presents Juliet as conflicted. Juliet's confused feelings about Romeo are illustrated in her use of oxymorons like "Beautiful tyrant". This suggests that Romeo is both "Beautiful" because he is her husband and a "tyrant" because he has killed her cousin. The way Juliet places opposing words next to each other emphasises the extreme nature of her conflict. Juliet's conflicted feelings highlight the difficulty of her situation to the audience and therefore illustrate her bravery and perseverance.
- Shakespeare presents Juliet as someone who is prepared to defend her beliefs. When the Nurse declares "Shame come to Romeo!", Juliet defends him, saying "Blistered be thy tongue". The vivid image of a blistered tongue creates an image of disease and makes it sound like Juliet is cursing the Nurse. This harsh tone contrasts with Juliet's usual respectful tone, emphasising how far she is prepared to go to defend her belief in Romeo's honour. The way that Juliet passionately defends her beliefs shows her maturity to the audience, especially as her adult tone contrasts with her youthful appearance on stage.
- Shakespeare presents Juliet as perceptive. She realises that Tybalt "would have killed my husband" had Romeo not killed him first. The audience already knows from the previous scene that Juliet is correct, which allows Shakespeare to highlight Juliet's insightful nature. The fact that Juliet is able to see a more nuanced version of the situation than the rest of her family would have encouraged a 16th-century audience to question the common assumption of the time that men were naturally more intelligent than women.

2. b)
- In Act 3, Scene 1, Romeo is loyal to Juliet by refusing to fight Tybalt, showing the strength of his love for her. Romeo tells Tybalt he will not fight him, claiming that he loves him "better than thou canst devise". The fact that Romeo has gone from hating Tybalt to loving him demonstrates that his loyalty to Juliet is now deeper than his loyalty to his family. This shows the strength of his love for her. However, this new loyalty is not presented as an easy choice. This is shown through Mercutio's shock at Romeo's refusal to fight, which suggests that Romeo's actions go against what is expected of him.
- Friar Lawrence's loyalty to Juliet is governed by religion and helps to drive the plot forward. In Act 4, Scene 1, he comes up with a "remedy" to help Juliet avoid committing a sin by marrying Paris. The word "remedy" is often used in relation to curing illness, which emphasises the fact that the Friar is acting to protect Juliet. However, his attempt to protect her enables her plan to fake her death, and ultimately contributes to her actual death. In the 16th century, many people feared that sinning would cause them to go to hell. As a religious figure, it is therefore Friar Lawrence's duty to prevent Juliet from sinning, even if it means deceiving Capulet and Lady Capulet.
- Paris's loyalty to Juliet suggests that his love is genuine. Before he tries to arrest Romeo in Act 5, Scene 3, Paris accuses him of coming to do "some villainous shame" on Juliet and Tybalt's tomb. The idea that 'shaming' Juliet is "villainous" to Paris demonstrates his loyalty to her, as he is defending her honour, even in death. This suggests that he really loved her. Paris's loyalty to Juliet makes the audience feel more sympathetic towards him than earlier in the play, as it shows that his motive for marrying Juliet wasn't simply desire for wealth and status.

3.
- Shakespeare presents Capulet as unpredictable. In this extract he "will make a desperate tender" in order for Juliet to marry Paris, whereas in Act 1, Scene 2, Capulet suggests that it is too soon for Juliet to marry. The word "desperate" shows how Capulet's views have changed, as it suggests he wants Juliet to marry Paris as a matter of urgency. The dramatic shift in Capulet's attitude emphasises his changeable nature to the audience. Capulet's unpredictable nature is also shown by the way he changes how he addresses Paris in the extract, first using the formal "sir" and then the more familiar "my son".
- Shakespeare presents Capulet as someone who is used to getting what he wants. In the extract, he asks Paris whether he is happy with the timing of the wedding after he has decided when it will take place. The fact Capulet uses short questions, "Will you be ready? Do you like this haste?", without waiting for Paris to answer suggests that his reply would be largely irrelevant. Capulet's assumed authority is reflected in the next scene when Juliet gives him an answer he doesn't like and Capulet reacts with shock.
- Shakespeare presents Capulet as protective of Juliet. In Act 1, Scene 2, Capulet says he does not want Paris to marry Juliet yet because she is "yet a stranger in the world". The word "stranger" suggests that the world is a place that Juliet does not know and is in danger of getting lost in. This implies that Capulet sees her as being vulnerable and in need of his protection. Capulet's desire to protect Juliet reflects family structures when Shakespeare wrote the play. Sons, daughters, and their husbands and wives were important to wealthy, upper-class fathers as a means of passing on wealth and power.

4.
- Mercutio is presented as arrogant in the way he provokes Tybalt. In the extract, Mercutio says he might "dry-beat" eight of Tybalt's "nine lives" out of him, which highlights his confidence that he could beat him severely if he wanted to. Traditionally, beating is a form of punishment, so Mercutio's threat also suggests that he sees Tybalt as being subordinate to him. The condescending tone of his threat would have had more significance for a 16th-century audience as, at that time, being socially inferior to someone often meant being worthy of less respect.
- Mercutio's arrogance is also shown in his refusal to back down in the extract. Romeo asks Mercutio to lower his sword, but Mercutio ignores him, telling Tybalt to "Come, sir". The fact that he doesn't answer Romeo suggests he is self-important; he has taken Tybalt's demand to duel Romeo so personally that he won't listen to reason. Mercutio's flamboyant, attention-seeking nature is also an important source of humour in the play, which gives it elements of a comedy.
- Mercutio mocks other people's beliefs. In Act 1, Scene 4, he makes fun of Romeo's opinion that dreams can be prophetic. He jokes that Queen Mab, "the fairies' midwife", rides in a chariot delivering dreams. His speech uses fairy-tale imagery, which implies that he thinks Romeo is being naive as fairy tales are usually associated with children. The arrogance in Mercutio's dismissal of Romeo's belief is emphasised by the structure of the play, as Romeo's dream in Act 5, Scene 1 does foreshadow events in Act 5, Scene 3. The way that Romeo kisses Juliet shortly before she wakes to find him dead echoes his vision of being brought back to life by a kiss from Juliet.

Section Three — Context and Themes

Page 31: Religion

1. rules, seriously, church, wedding, only, together
    (Other answers are also possible.)

2. b) E.g. Despite her fears, Juliet trusts Friar Lawrence because he works for the Church, which helps her to drink the potion.

68

Answers

c) E.g. The fact that suicide was seen as a sin shows how desperate Romeo and Juliet feel when they take their own lives.
3. E.g. Yes, because she says "Beshrew" (curse) her heart when she advises Juliet to marry Paris, which suggests that she knows it is a sinful thing to do but thinks it's in Juliet's best interests. **Or** e.g. No, because she's concerned about Juliet's happiness rather than her virtue. She says that Juliet's match to Paris "excels" her match to Romeo, even though marrying Paris would be immoral.
4. E.g. Confession is the only reason Juliet can leave her house unaccompanied.

Pages 32-33: Family and Marriage

1. a) E.g. "Be ruled by me, forget to think of her." (Act 1, Scene 1, line 219)
   b) E.g. "Doth she not give us thanks?" (Act 3, Scene 5, line 142)
2. E.g. He orders Tybalt not to harm Romeo at the party. / He threatens to throw Juliet out if she doesn't marry Paris.
3. E.g. Whoever married Juliet would be the sole heir to his wealth and reputation, so he would have been keen to find a noble husband who was responsible and respectable.
4. a) E.g. "Deny thy father and refuse thy name." (Act 2, Scene 2, line 34)
   b) E.g. "It fits when such a villain is a guest: / I'll not endure him." (Act 1, Scene 5, lines 74-75)
5. E.g. He requests Capulet's permission, as in the 16th century it was the father's responsibility to find his daughter a husband.
6. E.g. She got married when she was younger than Juliet, so she expects her to take the idea of marrying Paris seriously. She tries to persuade her about Paris's good qualities, as she believes that Juliet has reached an age where she should start to think about marriage.
7. E.g. In the 16th century, fathers usually found husbands for their daughters, and daughters were supposed to accept their father's chosen suitor. Modern audiences would generally find it normal for a woman to choose her husband.
8. E.g. "Have you got leave to go to shrift today?" (Act 2, Scene 5, line 66)
9. a) E.g. Yes, because he says "My blood for your rude brawls doth lie a-bleeding" when he gives out his sentence. The reference to "My blood" emphasises that his ties to Mercutio have influenced his decision. **Or** e.g. No. He makes his decision immediately after Montague speaks, so may have agreed with him that Romeo's actions weren't that unlawful, as Tybalt deserved to die because he had killed somebody.
   b) Quote: E.g. "He is a kinsman to the Montague / Affection makes him false". (Act 3, Scene 1, lines 172-173)
   Explanation: Lady Capulet suggests that because Benvolio and Romeo are family, Benvolio cannot be trusted to give a fair account of the fight.
Task: Here are some points you could have included:
   • Romeo is wealthy. This means he will be able to continue to provide Juliet with the quality of life that she has come to expect as a member of the Capulet family.
   • Romeo has Juliet's consent to marry her. This means she will be happy in her marriage, and Capulet will not have to continue the search for suitors who need to get his daughter's consent before marrying her.
   • Romeo is known throughout Verona as being "virtuous and well-governed". His positive reputation suggests that he will make a good husband for Juliet.

Page 34: Conflict, Honour and Feuds

1. E.g. Characters passionately uphold their honour and use violence to settle disputes. For example, Tybalt is passionate as he argues with Capulet, and requests a duel with Romeo to defend his honour.
2. E.g. To show the dangerous nature of the feud and emphasise to the audience how easily the conflict can turn violent.
3. You should have ticked the second and third statements.
4. E.g. Romeo doesn't fight Tybalt because of his love for Juliet. This conflicts with his ability to defend his honour, so Mercutio fights in his place.

5. E.g. Montague and Capulet realise it has led to their children's deaths.
Task: Here are some points you could have included:
   • Honour is an important cause of violence
     - In the extract, Tybalt wants to fight Romeo because he thinks he has mocked "our solemnity".
     - Tybalt wants to defend his family's honour, which leads to violence — shows how dangerous honour is.
     - Context — Shakespeare may have been inspired by Italian stereotypes when writing *Romeo and Juliet* (Italians = passionate).
   • Honour is a significant obstacle to Romeo and Juliet's love.
     - Romeo has to choose between his love for Juliet or his family honour in Act 3, Scene 1.
     - The fact Romeo gives in to honour and kills Tybalt shows he and Juliet cannot escape the family feud — power of honour.
     - Emphasised in the difference in Romeo's language at the start of the scene ("Doth much excuse the appertaining rage") and the end ("fire-eyed fury").
   • Family honour is the main cause of Romeo and Juliet hiding their love.
     - Juliet — "refuse they name" — shows she can't tell her parents about Romeo because he is from an enemy family.
     - Important as it causes Romeo and Juliet to keep their love a secret from their parents.
     - Emphasised in Act 3, Scene 5, when Lady Capulet wants "vengeance" for Tybalt, and Juliet uses double meanings to disguise her love.

Pages 35-36: Love

1. E.g. His love for Rosaline mimics courtly love. He writes clichéd love poetry for her and cares more about being in love than being with Rosaline herself. Romeo's love for Juliet is more realistic and being in love with her makes him feel happy.
2. a) E.g. Romeo is tormented by the fact that Rosaline won't love him.
   b) E.g. Rosaline says that she will not love Romeo, claiming she wants to remain a virgin.
   c) E.g. Romeo uses oxymorons like "heavy lightness" to describe his love with Rosaline.
3. E.g. Rosaline knew that Romeo's love for her wasn't true love. His knowledge of love was like something learnt "by rote", rather than something he knew well enough to "spell" out himself.
4. E.g. Some of Romeo's lines rhyme with Juliet's lines. This implies that they already identify with each other and complement one another, which demonstrates their closeness.
5. a) "It is enough I may but call her mine." (Act 2, Scene 6, line 8)
   b) "Leap to these arms". (Act 3, Scene 2, line 7)
6. E.g. When Shakespeare was writing, most daughters from rich families married the person their fathers chose, not for love.
7. E.g. Quote: "seek happy nights to happy days." (Act 1, Scene 3, line 106)
   Explanation: E.g. To contrast other characters' purely physical views of love with Romeo and Juliet's true love. Rude jokes about sex make love seem crude, which highlights the purity of Romeo and Juliet's love.
8. E.g. Death is present in Romeo and Juliet's relationship from the start of the play, when the prologue states the "lovers" will "take their life". This link is continued throughout the play through the characters' dialogue, for example, Romeo says that death is "love-devouring".

Page 37: Fate

1. E.g. "Star-crossed" suggests that their love is doomed, while "misadventured piteous overthrows" suggests they will die.
2. E.g. "O, I am fortune's fool." (Act 3, Scene 1, line 132) / "I defy you, stars!" (Act 5, Scene 1, line 24)
3. E.g. Yes, because asking Romeo to marry her so quickly leads to a conflict with Paris's proposal. This creates the need for a plan for Juliet to escape, which leads to her suicide. **Or** e.g. No, because it is Romeo's actions that force him to go to Mantua, and it is the failure of the Friar's message that leads to Romeo's suicide. This suggests that other factors are more influential.

Answers

4.	E.g. It has control over characters. For example, Romeo blames fate for causing Tybalt's death in Act 3, Scene 1.
5.	E.g. To make the audience think more deeply about whether our actions are controlled by fate, or whether we have the free will to decide our own futures.

Exam Practice:

Your answer should have an introduction, several paragraphs developing different ideas and a conclusion. You may have covered some of the following points:

- Fate is an important source of tension in the play. In this extract, Romeo says he fears that due to the fate "hanging in the stars", going to the party will cause his "untimely death". The verb "hanging" gives the impression of something dangling above Romeo, ready to fall. This creates tension, as it implies that Romeo is in constant danger. It also creates suspense, as it reminds the audience that Romeo and Juliet will die by the end of the play but gives no indication of when it will happen.
- Fate allows Shakespeare to explore ideas about blame. In Act 3, Scene 1, Romeo says that he is "fortune's fool" for killing Tybalt. This suggests that he belongs to fortune, which highlights his belief that he is being controlled by fate. However, earlier in the scene Romeo declares that his actions are being driven by anger. This contradiction challenges the audience to decide whether fate or characters' actions have a bigger role in the play. Uncertainty about blame is also explored at the end of the play when Friar Lawrence, whose unsuccessful plan helped lead to Romeo and Juliet's deaths, blames a "greater power" for their downfall.
- The inevitable nature of fate makes the play more tragic. When Romeo hears of Juliet's death in Act 5, Scene 1, he tries to "defy" fate by returning to Verona to kill himself. However, his death is fated, so by killing himself Romeo actually fulfils his destiny. This highlights how trapped Romeo is, as even when he tries to challenge fate, he fails. His death therefore seems more tragic. This sense of helplessness is also evident in the way Juliet is trapped by the demands of her family. In the 16th century, unmarried daughters in wealthy families were expected to abide by their fathers' rules. This limits Juliet's power in the play, which reflects her inability to escape her fate.

Page 38: Writing about Context

1. a)	The idea that the father should be the authority figure within the family would have been familiar to an audience in the 16th century and would have made Juliet's decision to marry Romeo without her parent's permission seem more rebellious.
   b)	In Shakespeare's time, many people would have considered it sinful for an unmarried couple to live or sleep together.
2.	Piece of context: 2
   Explanation of choice: The P.E.E.D. bullets show how worried Juliet feels about the prospect of having to marry a second man. The second piece of context explains why this would have been significant to Shakespeare's audience.

Page 39: Practice Questions

Your answers should have an introduction, several paragraphs developing different ideas and a conclusion. You may have covered some of the following points:

1.	• Love is presented as purely sexual by some characters in the play. In Act 2, Scene 1, Mercutio describes Rosaline using body parts, like her "quivering thigh". Mercutio's language draws attention to her physical features, which suggests his attitude to love is mainly sexual. His vulgar attitude towards love is important to the form of the play, as it provides a source of comedy. This is emphasised by the way the play's mood becomes more serious (like a typical tragedy) after his death.
   • Romeo's attitude towards love is shaped by ignorance. In the extract, Benvolio remarks that Romeo's love is "Blind". The word "Blind" implies that Romeo has no idea what he is looking for when it comes to love, suggesting that his attitude towards love is characterised by a lack of knowledge. This is supported by the way Romeo tries to pursue Rosaline using the traditions of courtly love, a medieval method of courtship. The fact that he tries to woo her using learnt methods shows that

his attitude towards love isn't driven by his own instincts.
- Both Romeo and Juliet view love as a strong commitment. This is shown in Act 2, Scene 2, when Juliet refers to Romeo as a "tassel-gentle" (a falcon) and Romeo calls Juliet a "niësse" (a young hawk). This falconry metaphor suggests that Romeo and Juliet consider themselves to be strongly attached to one another now they're in love, because they return to each other as a bird returns to its falconer. This metaphor also highlights the equality in Romeo and Juliet's love, as neither of them sees the other as their 'handler'.

2.	• Religion is an important part of the predicament Juliet finds herself in when she is told to marry Paris. In this extract, Juliet says that her husband is "on earth" and her faith is "in heaven". This suggests that only divine intervention could dissolve Juliet's marriage to Romeo and prevent her from committing a sin. The size of the problem is emphasised by the juxtaposition of "heaven" and "earth"; the fact that Juliet is faced with trying to reconcile two contrasting ideas shows the impossibility of her predicament. The serious nature of her dilemma would have been more apparent to a 16th-century audience, as many of them would have believed that Juliet would go to hell for marrying Paris.
   • Religious practices are used as important plot devices in the play. In this extract and earlier in the play, Juliet leaves her house to "make confession" at Friar Lawrence's cell. The solitary and confidential nature of confession allows Shakespeare to use it as a means of Juliet seeking help and continuing her relationship with Romeo. Confidentiality is part of the reason Friar Lawrence is unable to tell the Capulets what has happened, as his religious vows mean he has to respect Juliet's confidence.
   • Religion is an important source of trust in the play. In Act 4, Scene 3, Juliet is worried that the Friar intends to poison her with the potion, but decides to trust him because he has been "tried a holy man". This suggests that being a member of the Church makes Friar Lawrence seem more trustworthy. The link between religion and trust is echoed at the end of the play when the Prince indicates that Friar Lawrence won't be punished for his role in Romeo's and Juliet's deaths, because the Prince considers him to be "a holy man".

3.	• In this extract, Shakespeare presents the feud as a cause of misery. Upon seeing Romeo and Juliet's dead bodies, Capulet exclaims "O heavens!" while Montague asks "What manners is in this?" This exclamation and rhetorical question show the shock and distress that the fathers of both families feel upon seeing their children dead as a result of their feud. The misery shown in this extract echoes the distress of characters in Act 3 following Tybalt's death and Romeo's banishment, reinforcing the idea that the feud causes misery among both the Montagues and the Capulets.
   • In this extract, Shakespeare presents the feud as widespread. Shakespeare structures the scene so that the order of when characters appear on stage is staggered, with different characters learning of the deaths at different times. This means the number of people affected by the feud is emphasised because it is presented gradually. This use of staging would be particularly striking for an audience watching the play, as by the end of the scene there would be a lot of people on stage together, highlighting the extensive impact of the feud.
   • Elsewhere in the play, the feud is presented as an obstacle to Romeo and Juliet's love. In Act 1, Scene 5, Juliet recognises that her one true love has "sprung from" her "only hate". This shows that her love for Romeo is inseparably linked to the family conflict, which suggests that the feud will always come between them. The idea of the family feud being an obstacle to her love for Romeo is also shown in Act 3, Scene 5, when Juliet rejects her father's choice of husband in order to be loyal to Romeo. This would have been a difficult decision in the 16th century, when the consequences for a girl losing her family were serious, as family was an important source of protection, support and financial security.

Answers

4. a) • In this extract, Juliet and her father's relationship mimics one based on the typical family structures of the time. Juliet tells Capulet "I beseech you! / Henceforward I am ever ruled by you." The repetition of "you" emphasises the idea that Juliet's life revolves around her father's wishes and reveals Juliet's attempt to deceive her father into thinking she has submitted to his will to marry Paris. A 16th-century audience may have been shocked by her behaviour, as daughters then were expected to be obedient to their fathers' wishes.
    • The relationship between Juliet and her father is presented as loving, but only when Juliet is obedient. At the end of the extract, Capulet remarks "My heart is wondrous light" because he thinks Juliet obeys him. This suggests that Capulet now feels like a weight has been lifted from his heart. His description implies that he no longer sees Juliet as a burden and that his love for her is once again unhindered. However, the fact he then says that this is because she has been "reclaimed" suggests his love is conditional on her obedience. This idea is echoed in Act 3, Scene 5, Lady Capulet tells Juliet that she is "done with" her because of her refusal to marry Paris.
    • The relationship between Juliet and her father is presented as unbalanced, as Capulet has much more power than Juliet. The fact that Capulet is able to move the wedding forward to "tomorrow morning" without considering Juliet shows Juliet's lack of power compared to Capulet, suggesting that he holds the authority in their relationship. This is emphasised by how short the scene is, which highlights that events move at the speed Capulet wants them to, without regard for Juliet.
   b) • Shakespeare shows that, for Romeo and Juliet, marriage is an integral part of love. In Act 2, Scene 2, Juliet tells Romeo that "If thou dost love, pronounce it faithfully." The verb "pronounce" is often used in wedding ceremonies to signify the marriage of two people. This shows the link in Juliet's mind between love and marriage, which could explain her eagerness to marry Romeo so soon after they meet. This connection is emphasised by the fact that the qualities of Romeo and Juliet's love are reflected in their wedding ceremony. In Act 2, Scene 6, the couple's wedding is "short", which mirrors the short-lived nature of their love as a whole.
    • Shakespeare shows that marriage isn't just for love. In Act 1, Scene 3, Lady Capulet presents Paris as a potential suitor for Juliet, describing the "delight" in his handsome features and calling him "precious". Her persuasive language reveals her excitement at the idea of their marriage, even though Juliet doesn't love Paris. Lady Capulet's enthusiasm towards Paris might be because finding a wealthy and well-regarded husband for Juliet is important to her. This was characteristic of the views of many rich people in the 16th century, who often married to secure money or social status.
    • Shakespeare presents marriage as sacred. In Act 4, Scene 1, Juliet says that she is willing to face her fears in order to live "unstained" by not marrying Paris. The word "unstained" suggests Juliet believes that she will forever be marked if she marries Paris after already marrying Romeo. This reflects the idea that marriage is a sacred bond that cannot be broken without serious negative consequences, which causes Juliet to follow the Friar's risky plan. The sacredness of marriage in the play demonstrates the fact that marriage was generally seen as a lifetime commitment approved by God at the time Shakespeare was writing.

Section Four — Shakespeare's Techniques

Pages 40-41: Form and Structure of 'Romeo and Juliet'

1. E.g. Yes, because when Romeo hears that Juliet is dead, his reckless nature leads him to immediately buy poison and go to the Capulet tomb to kill himself. **Or** e.g. No, because the fact that Friar Lawrence's letter doesn't reach Romeo causes the misunderstanding about Juliet's death, which motivates Romeo to kill himself.
2. E.g. There are lots of entrances and exits, which makes it seem busy because they create a lot of movement on stage.

3. b) E.g. It creates tension, as the audience knows that Romeo won't be around to help Juliet.
   c) E.g. It provides some comic relief for the audience as the mood goes from being very serious to light-hearted.
   d) E.g. It creates suspense as the audience wonders whether Romeo will learn the truth before he reaches Juliet's tomb.
4. E.g. He warns that "they stumble that run fast". Romeo's haste to marry Juliet and to return to Verona is partly to blame for his death.
5. E.g. To speed up the pace of the play. This faster pace emphasises the way that Juliet is being pushed into marrying Paris and gives the impression that events are beginning to speed out of control.
6. a) This creates suspense because the audience knows that any future fighting will have very serious consequences.
   b) The audience knows that it's likely that Paris and Romeo will meet, and waits in suspense to see Paris's reaction to Romeo.
7. E.g. To create tension, as the audience wonders how much worse the violence will get and who will be hurt next.
8. E.g. Mercutio's death, because it leads to Romeo's banishment. The way he is distanced from other characters allows important misunderstandings to take place, which contribute to the play's tragic ending. **Or** e.g. Juliet's decision to fake her own death, because if she hadn't done this, Romeo might not have killed himself, which means that Juliet might not have killed herself either.

Task: Here are some points you may have included for Juliet appearing at a window above Romeo:
    • Positioning her above Romeo makes his comparison between Juliet and an angel seem stronger. It reflects the fact that he feels she has come from heaven.
    • The fact that Juliet can't go down to the orchard but has to speak to Romeo through the window of her parents' house suggests that she's confined by her position as Capulet's daughter.
Here are some points you may have included for Juliet kneeling down before Capulet:
    • This action emphasises the fact that Juliet is begging Capulet. It makes Juliet seem humble, and makes Capulet, who continues to speak angrily to her, seem unreasonable to the audience.
    • Juliet knows that kneeling before Capulet will make him feel more powerful because it shows him respect. This suggests that she is intelligent and knows how to influence people.

Page 42: Mood and Atmosphere

1. E.g. Both prologues remind the audience that Romeo and Juliet's love is dangerous. For example, the Prologue to Act 1 says it is "death-marked". This creates an ominous mood, as the audience wonders how and when this danger will unfold.
2. b) E.g. It highlights Romeo and Juliet's need for secrecy, which creates a tense atmosphere.
   c) E.g. It creates an uneasy atmosphere, because it is a public place where fighting is forbidden, but the hot weather means characters are more likely to be irritable. This increases the chance of conflict.
3. E.g. The repetition of "most" and "ever" emphasises the idea that the Nurse has never experienced such grief before, creating a sorrowful atmosphere.
4. E.g. It becomes darker and more serious as there are fewer jokes and innuendos to lighten the mood.

Exam Practice:
    Your answer should have an introduction, several paragraphs developing different ideas and a conclusion.
    You may have covered some of the following points:
    • Shakespeare creates a light-hearted atmosphere in this extract through his use of prose (unrhymed sentences without a set rhythm). Shakespeare often used blank verse for upper-class characters and serious topics, and prose for lower-class characters and lighter topics. Despite Mercutio's upper-class status, Shakespeare makes him speak in prose in this extract. This signals that Mercutio's comments should not be taken seriously. Prose also contributes to the light-hearted

Answers

atmosphere earlier in Act 2, Scene 4, in which Romeo and Mercutio exchange playful jokes.

- A light-hearted atmosphere is also created through Mercutio's use of mockery. He describes the "new tuners of accents" (those who use the latest slang) as "strange flies". This suggests that, rather than sounding impressive, the language the fashionable men use is irritating and monotonous, like the buzzing of a fly. By making this comparison, Shakespeare exaggerates how annoying slang and its users are, creating humour. Topical references like this would have seemed particularly funny in the 16th century, as audience members would have recognised the sort of people being mocked.

- A humorous atmosphere is created in Act 1, Scene 3 through the rambling nature of the Nurse's speech. The Nurse keeps interrupting her own story, adding irrelevant bits in before coming back to her point with the words "but, as I said". The Nurse's poor story-telling highlights her scatterbrained nature to the audience, encouraging them to laugh at her. Furthermore, humour is created in this scene through the way the Nurse uses vulgar, sexual language about Juliet in a conversation with her mother. Her lack of awareness about the inappropriateness of this conversation topic provides entertainment for the audience.

Page 43: Dramatic Irony

1. E.g. Juliet is excited about her upcoming wedding night, but the audience knows that Romeo has just been banished so it might not happen.
2. a) E.g. The audience knows straight away that their relationship is dangerous. This makes the audience feel tense.
   b) E.g. The audience waits in suspense to see whether Juliet will wake up in time to stop Romeo from killing himself.
3. The audience knows that Juliet is alive. By killing himself, Romeo thinks he is ending his misfortune, but is unaware that his actions are actually going to create more problems.
4. E.g. It makes the audience feel more involved in the play. For example, they might feel more concerned for Juliet in the last act of the play because they know that she is fated to die.

Page 44: Poetry in Shakespeare

1. E.g. "This letter doth make good the Friar's words, / Their course of love, the tidings of her death". (Act 5, Scene 3, lines 286-287)
2. E.g. It suggests that their feelings are mutual and that loving each other comes naturally to them.
3. a) E.g. It emphasises the idea that Capulet is too old to be fighting.
   b) E.g. Pauses and short phrases create an uneven rhythm. This makes it seem like the action is moving quickly and uncontrollably.
4. E.g. Quote: "Why dost thou stay?" (line 132)
   Explanation: The short words make the pace of the passage quick, which adds to the tense atmosphere.
5. E.g. To make the audience feel sorry for him. His soliloquy gives him the opportunity to go into detail about his sorrow.

Page 45: Puns and Wordplay

1. meaning, pronounced, funny, entertain
2. E.g. To insult Tybalt. Mercutio deliberately misinterprets Tybalt, then mocks him for his choice of words in an attempt to provoke him into fighting.
3. E.g. Juliet uses an ambiguous word to trick her mother into thinking she hates Romeo, rather than loves him. The fact Lady Capulet can't tell shows her distant relationship with Juliet.
4. E.g. It suggests that they are close, because it shows that they can tease each other without causing any offence.
Task: Here are some puns you might have chosen:
- In Act 2, Scene 4, Mercutio says, "an old hare hoar" (lines 115-116). 'Hoar' can mean 'mouldy', but sounds the same as 'whore'. This rude pun helps to create a light-hearted mood and entertains the audience.
- In Act 1, Scene 4, Mercutio tells Romeo to "borrow Cupid's wings, / And soar with them above a common bound", suggesting that because Romeo is a lover he can use Cupid's

wings to rise above to where others cannot 'leap'. However, Romeo replies that he is "bound" (lines 17-18) meaning that he is tied down. This pun contrasts Mercutio's optimism with Romeo's negative attitude and emphasises the difference between them at this point in the play.
- In Act 1, Scene 1, Samson and Gregory use the words "choler" (anger) and "collar" (hangman's noose), which are homophones (words that sound the same). By linking anger to the noose, Shakespeare hints that the characters' anger could lead to death. This creates a tense mood.

Pages 46-47: Imagery and Symbolism

1. E.g. Romeo personifies love by giving it negative human qualities like being "rude" and "boisterous". It is as if he's being bullied by love, which suggests that it is cruel.
2. E.g. To show how hard Lady Capulet is trying to convince Juliet of Paris's good qualities. The extended metaphor allows her to showcase Paris's features in great detail.
3. a) E.g. "dear saint" (line 102) / "Give me my sin again." (line 109)
   b) E.g. It suggests their relationship is pure. It also implies that their love is so strong that it borders on worship.
4. E.g. In Act 2, Scene 2, Romeo says he would sail "the farthest sea" to reach Juliet, but in Act 5, Scene 3, Romeo says he will crash on "The dashing rocks". The imagery becomes more bleak, which highlights how Romeo has lost hope and become more desperate.
5. b) E.g. "Spread thy close curtain, love-performing night". (Act 3, Scene 2, line 5)
   The link Juliet draws between her love for Romeo and darkness reminds the audience of the need for secrecy in their relationship.
   c) E.g. The way the darkness takes over emphasises how the feud has put out the light of their love.
6. true, false, false, true
7. E.g. Juliet wishes the Nurse were "as swift in motion as a ball" but instead she is "heavy and pale as lead." The contrast between a ball and lead helps the reader to understand Juliet's frustration.
8. E.g. The image suggests that Juliet has died too early, as frost is associated with winter but she is still in the 'springtime' of her life. In the play, time often works against the characters, particularly Romeo and Juliet.

Page 48: Working with Extracts

1. E.g. In the previous scene, Paris asked Capulet's permission to marry Juliet. In the next scene, Romeo, Mercutio and Benvolio are going to Capulet's party.
2. E.g. Lady Capulet believes that Juliet will complete Paris, like a cover completes a book.
3. E.g. The perfect rhyming couplets suggest that Lady Capulet believes Paris would make a perfect husband for Juliet.
4. E.g. In Act 4, Scene 5, the Nurse tells Juliet to sleep because she will "rest but little" on her wedding night.

Page 49: Practice Questions

Your answers should have an introduction, several paragraphs developing different ideas and a conclusion. You may have covered some of the following points:
1.
- Juliet's questions create a tense atmosphere in this extract. She worries not only about whether the potion will work, but also about what will happen if she wakes up before Romeo arrives. Juliet's questions highlight the risks of her actions, which makes the audience fear for her. This scene is made more tense through Shakespeare's staging. Juliet is alone on stage at this point, which means that there is no one to break the tension by reassuring her or the audience that the plan will work.
- Shakespeare uses the structure of Act 4 to create a tense atmosphere. Juliet drinks the potion in Scene 3, but her body is not discovered by her household until Scene 5. This use of dramatic irony means that the audience knows that Juliet's body could be discovered at any moment, but is held in suspense until Scene 5. Dramatic irony is also a source

Answers

of tension in the final scene of the play, when the audience knows that Romeo has killed himself but is forced to watch as Juliet discovers his death for herself.

- The setting of Act 5, Scene 3 creates a tense atmosphere. Friar Lawrence draws attention to the eerie nature of the churchyard by talking about "eyeless skulls". The word "skulls" reminds the audience of the dead bodies in the graveyard, and the addition of "eyeless" emphasises this image of decay in the audience members' minds. This makes the scene feel sinister. Graphic descriptions like this would have been particularly important in the 16th century, when limited staging options meant that the atmosphere of the setting often had to be conveyed through the characters' dialogue, rather than through lighting or props.

2.
- In the extract, Shakespeare hints to the audience that Romeo and Juliet's relationship is doomed through the way the news of Juliet's death makes Romeo "wild". The word "wild" makes it seem as though Romeo is an animal, having lost his sense of reason. The audience already knows that recklessness is Romeo's weakness and therefore fears that he will act rashly and put Friar Lawrence's plan to save both him and Juliet in danger. The idea that Romeo's 'wild' nature contributes to the play's tragic ending is reinforced when he tells Paris that his plans are "savage-wild" during their confrontation by the tomb.
- The tragic form of the play makes Romeo and Juliet's relationship seem doomed. In many tragedies, the main character's death is inevitable, so a 16th-century audience would have considered it likely that Romeo and Juliet's relationship would end in their untimely deaths. However, unlike many tragedies, the deaths of the tragic hero and heroine in *Romeo and Juliet* isn't necessarily a result of their own fatal flaws. Fate arguably plays a greater role in Romeo and Juliet's deaths.
- Shakespeare uses the Chorus to show that Romeo and Juliet cannot escape their fate. In the Prologue to Act 1, the Chorus states that their love is "death-marked". By setting out the events of the play before the action has even begun, Shakespeare gives the impression that Romeo and Juliet are trapped by the play's structure, and are therefore doomed. Choruses are often used in tragedies to guide the audience through the events of the play, so the audience is likely to consider the information they give about Romeo and Juliet's tragic destinies to be reliable.

3.
- Shakespeare presents Paris as a loving character through his use of verse in this extract. When he is left alone, he speaks in rhymed verse. This slows down the pace of the scene, which makes him sound melancholy, suggesting that the love he expresses for Juliet is heartfelt. Shakespeare may have chosen to explore Paris's loving nature just before his death to create sympathy for him, by making it clear that he has lost someone he loved.
- The way that Shakespeare structures Act 5, Scene 3 encourages the audience to compare Paris with Romeo. The characters arrive at the churchyard straight after one another, accompanied by servants who are carrying torches, and both then ask their servants to hand over their torches and give them privacy. The repetition of this sequence of events encourages the audience to see the similarities between Paris and Romeo. The similarities between Romeo and Paris are emphasised by Paris' request to die "with Juliet", which is also what Romeo wants for himself.
- Paris is presented as a powerful character through the way other characters address him. Capulet uses "you" instead of "thou" when he speaks to Paris in Act 3, Scene 4. In the 16th century, "you" was used to show respect to someone of high social status, so its use indicates that Capulet recognises Paris as a powerful character. The way that other characters such as Friar Lawrence often refer to Paris using his title "County" reinforces the idea that Paris is an important character of high social standing.

4. a)
- In this passage, Shakespeare suggests that Mercutio cares about Romeo. He tries to cheer Romeo up, saying "we must

have you dance". The use of the word "must" shows that Mercutio's attempt to cheer Romeo up is forceful, and therefore demonstrates how much he cares about Romeo. The audience already knows from Act 1, Scene 1 that Romeo feels as though he has "lost" himself, which makes Mercutio's caring nature at this point in the play more valuable.

- Shakespeare suggests that the relationship between Romeo and Mercutio is one-sided in this extract. Romeo continually rejects Mercutio's attempts to raise his spirits. For example, after Mercutio urges Romeo to "soar" with Cupid's wings, Romeo uses wordplay in his claim that being pierced by Cupid's arrow has made him "sore". The way Romeo gives Mercutio's words a negative connotation shows his refusal to engage with Mercutio's attempt to raise his spirits. The balance in their relationship is restored after Romeo has met Juliet; following some exchanges in which Romeo responds playfully, Mercutio comments "now art thou Romeo".
- In this extract, Romeo and Mercutio's closeness is shown by the way they use humour. Throughout the extract, they make puns on each others' words. For example, Romeo complains that love feels like it "pricks like a thorn", which Mercutio turns into a sexual pun by saying "Prick love for pricking". This shows that they are gently making fun of each other, which gives the impression that their friendship is close. Puns were a common way of introducing humour in 16th-century drama, so an audience in Shakespeare's time would have found the characters of Romeo and Mercutio particularly engaging.

b)
- Shakespeare uses settings to develop ideas about gender roles. Outdoor scenes are mainly dominated by male characters, whereas scenes involving Juliet, Lady Capulet and the Nurse are often set inside, mainly in Capulet's mansion. This division could reflect the common idea in the 16th century that men were free to engage in politics and conflict while women had little influence outside the home. This would have made Juliet's visits to Friar Lawrence's cell seem rebellious to an audience in Shakespeare's time, as she doesn't only disobey her parents, but also challenges her position as a young woman.
- The setting of Act 3, Scene 1 prepares the audience for the brawl that will unfold. Right at the start of the scene, Benvolio comments twice on the "hot" day. By including references to the heat twice in three lines, Shakespeare suggests that the heat, as well as the brawl that Benvolio warns of, are inescapable. The idea that the weather is partly to blame for the characters' short tempers makes them seem less responsible for their actions and suggests that some other force, possibly fate, might be in control of their destinies.
- Shakespeare uses the setting of the play's final scene to make the ending seem more tragic. At the end of the play, the discussion between various characters about why Romeo and Juliet have died takes place in the Capulets' tomb. Using the tomb as the setting acts as a constant visual reminder to the audience of the lives wasted as a result of the feud, especially as the bodies remain on stage until the end of the play. The way that Capulet and Montague are shown to resolve the feud between their families over the bodies of their children emphasises the wasteful loss of life.

Section Five — Exam Buster

Page 50: Understanding the Question

1. b) Write about the significance of religion in *Romeo and Juliet*.
   c) Explain how the relationship between Romeo and Mercutio is presented.
   d) How does Shakespeare explore attitudes to marriage in *Romeo and Juliet*?
   e) Write about the significance of Friar Lawrence in *Romeo and Juliet*.
   f) How is the character of the Nurse presented in *Romeo and Juliet*?
   g) Explain how the relationship between the Montague family and the Capulet family is presented.

2. a - 2, b - 1, c - 5, d - 3, e - 4

Answers

Page 51: Making a Rough Plan

1. E.g. Capulet personifies death to emphasise that he has no heir now that Juliet is dead. / Tybalt tries to fight Romeo to defend the honour of his family. / Juliet's loyalty to her family conflicts with her desire to be with Romeo.

2. Pick your three most important points and put them in a sensible order. Write down a quote or an example from the text to back up each one.

Page 52: Making Links

1. E.g. The Nurse uses a sexual pun when she refers to Juliet's wedding night in Act 4, Scene 5.
   In Act 2, Scene 4, the Nurse warns Romeo not to take advantage of Juliet.
   She betrays Juliet by condoning her marriage to Romeo, then changing her mind later on.

2. E.g. If one of your points was 'Juliet's loyalty to her family conflicts with her desire to be with Romeo', and your evidence was that Juliet asks Romeo to "refuse thy name", another example could be that she says "My only love sprung from my only hate", which suggests that Juliet thinks her loyalty to her family is an obstacle to her love for Romeo.

Page 53: Structuring Your Answer

1. Point: The feud between the families is shown to be extreme.
   Example: In Act 3, Scene 1, Benvolio worries that the weather during "these hot days" will provoke a brawl.
   Explain: The idea that something as mundane as hot weather could spark violence between the families suggests that the feud has gone past reason.
   Develop: As a result, Romeo's and Juliet's deaths seem particularly unnecessary and tragic to the audience.

2. a) Friar Lawrence thinks Romeo is "wedded to calamity".
   b) Juliet is "blubbering" because of Romeo's banishment.

3. E.g. Point: Tybalt tries to fight Romeo to defend the honour of his family.
   Example: In Act 1, Scene 5, he says that the way Romeo is mocking "our solemnity" justifies his murder.
   Explain: Tybalt's use of "our" instead of "your" shows his strong sense of family identity, and the fact that he believes Romeo's actions warrant his death shows how important defending his family's honour is to him.
   Develop: Tybalt's deep sense of loyalty to his family is illustrated in Act 3, Scene 1, when he dies defending his family's honour.

Page 54: Introductions and Conclusions

1. Intro a) is better, e.g. Intro b) does not present a judgement on how far Friar Lawrence is responsible. It also makes points that aren't relevant to the question, like the importance of religion to the play.

2. E.g. The conclusion should focus on Friar Lawrence, rather than on the Nurse. The third sentence shouldn't introduce new ideas and should be more relevant to the question. It should include a judgement about the 'extent' to which Friar Lawrence is presented as responsible.

Task: Your introduction and conclusion should both give a clear answer to the question. The introduction should include your main points, but no evidence. Your conclusion should summarise your argument and not include new points.

Page 55: Writing about Context

1. a - 2, b - 3, c - 1

2. Contextual information: In the 16th century, Shakespeare's plays were watched by people of all classes, so some audience members would have been illiterate. Including sexual innuendos was therefore an effective way for playwrights to entertain the whole audience at that time.

3. You could have included context as the Explain or Develop part of the paragraph. The context you wrote about should be relevant to your Point and linked to the Example.

Page 56: Linking Ideas and Paragraphs

1. E.g. Shakespeare indicates that Romeo and Juliet's marriage is ill-fated. In Act 2, Scene 6, just before they get married, Friar Lawrence says that even the "sweetest honey" becomes "loathsome" when it's eaten in excess. This suggests that Romeo and Juliet's happiness won't last. Similarly, In Act 3, Scene 3, Friar Lawrence says Romeo is "wedded to calamity".

2. You should have used the P.E.E.D. structure and included connecting words and phrases such as 'therefore' or 'which shows that' to link your ideas.

3. E.g. Moreover... / This idea is reinforced by...

Page 57: Marking Answer Extracts

1. 4-5: The answer gives a thoughtful response, but there are some spelling errors. It examines how Shakespeare uses language, but doesn't analyse it closely enough for it to be a 6-7 answer. The answer includes some contextual information, but this information isn't used to explore the relationship between the text and the play's context.

Page 58: Marking Answer Extracts

1. a) 8-9: E.g. "Here, the repetition of sharp 't' sounds... makes Tybalt seem threatening." — close and perceptive analysis of language
   "Tybalt's aggression... Romeo reacts with 'love.'" — arguments supported with well-integrated, precise examples from the text

   b) 6-7: E.g. "For example, Benvolio... 'deaf to peace'." — integrated, well-chosen examples
   "In the 16th century... in Shakespeare's time." — exploration of the relationship between the text and its context

Pages 59-60: Marking a Whole Answer

1. 8-9: E.g. The answer includes well-integrated, precise examples of how Shakespeare uses language, structure and form to convey ideas to the reader. There is a critical discussion of the relationship between the text and its social and historical context. The answer is well-written and uses highly relevant subject terminology.

Page 61: Writing Well

1. Friar Lawrence is a [an] important figure because his actions affect the plot. For instants [instance], he helps Romeo and Juliet to get married and gave [gives] Juliet the drug that makes her appear dead. Dispite [Despite] his good intentions, these actions contribute to the plays [play's] tragic ending. This makes it unclear whether Shakespeare wants the audience to see him as helpful or irresponsable [irresponsible].

2. a - 5, b - 4, c - 1, d - 3, e - 6, f - 2

Page 62: Practice Questions

Your answers should have an introduction, several paragraphs developing different ideas and a conclusion. You may have covered some of the following points:

1. a) • The extract shows the audience that Juliet is already certain about her love for Romeo at this point in the play. Juliet says she wants Romeo to remove his name and in its place "Take all myself." The word "all" shows her passion for Romeo, because it suggests that she already wants to give him everything. The fact that Juliet displays such a strong passion for Romeo after only just meeting him suggests that she is an immature character with little or no experience of love.

   • The extract shows that Juliet feels conflicted about her love for an enemy. Throughout this soliloquy, she repeats "name", "Romeo" and "Montague". This shows her fixation with the fact that she and Romeo come from opposite sides of the feud between their families. Shakespeare is able to show Juliet's feelings directly to the audience using a soliloquy. It allows her to honestly express her inner conflict.

   • The extract shows that Juliet's love for Romeo has overtaken her loyalty to her family. Juliet says that, if Romeo wants to keep his name, then she will "no longer be a Capulet." Despite the feud between their families, she is willing to reject hers to be with her love. For a young, unmarried woman to abandon her family in such a way would have shocked a Shakespearean audience, as at the time daughters were expected to stay with their family until their father found them a suitable husband.

b) • Shakespeare uses violence to establish how important the feud is to the play. Structuring the play so that there is a fight scene involving many characters at the very beginning (in Act 1, Scene 1) gives the audience an immediate insight into how extensive the feud is. In the 16th century, Italy was seen as a place where there was a lot of conflict. Shakespeare's decision to set the play in an Italian city therefore stresses the importance of violence to the play.

• Violence is important to the play as a way for characters to defend their honour. In Act 1, Scene 5, Tybalt says that killing Romeo at the party would not be "a sin" because it would defend the "honour of my kin". By using a rhyming couplet here, Shakespeare makes Tybalt's view seem final and indisputable. It gives the impression that, in Tybalt's view, it is always acceptable to use violence to defend honour. The connection between violence and honour is also highlighted later in the play, when Mercutio labels Romeo's refusal to fight Tybalt as "dishonourable".

• Violence is important to the play because it increases tension by creating a sense of panic amongst the characters. For example, the violence in Act 3, Scene 1 causes Benvolio to panic, saying "Romeo, away, be gone!" Benvolio normally speaks in iambic pentameter, so the fact that he uses a shorter line here shows his frantic state. Benvolio's panic increases the tension because it implies that the violence has led to events spiralling out of control. The violence also leads to a lot of characters coming on stage. This adds to the tension, as it suggests to the audience that the fight between Romeo and Tybalt is an important event which will have a wide impact on the play.

2. • Romeo is presented as immature in love. In the extract, Friar Lawrence remarks at how many wasted tears have fallen down Romeo's "sallow cheeks" as he cried about Rosaline. The word "sallow" suggests Romeo has cried so much that he looks unwell. This extreme reaction seems disproportionate, which implies that Romeo's feelings for Rosaline are immature. Romeo's immaturity is also emphasised by the way Juliet mocks him because he kisses "by th'book", suggesting that he has only read about kissing rather than experienced it himself.

• Romeo is presented as immature through the way he reacts to other characters. In Act 3, Scene 3, he argues that Friar Lawrence can't "speak" of what he doesn't "feel". Romeo's arrogant assumption that Friar Lawrence's advice isn't valuable because the Friar can't understand what he's experiencing highlights his immaturity. The immature way Romeo dismisses Friar Lawrence would have been especially apparent to a 16th-century audience, as they would have had great respect and trust in religious figures like the Friar.

• Romeo is shown to be reckless, which demonstrates his immaturity. In Act 5, Scene 1, after passing on the news of Juliet's death, Balthasar cautions Romeo not to act rashly. Romeo replies "Tush", curtly dismissing Balthasar's attempt to calm him down. This shows that Romeo is acting in haste, rather than stopping to assess the situation. Romeo's recklessness is further highlighted by the way he completes Balthasar's line, which gives the impression that he is interrupting Balthasar. This suggests that he is not even really listening to Balthasar's advice.

3. • Benvolio is presented as being loyal to Romeo. When he gives the Prince his account of the fight, he emphasises Romeo's peaceful behaviour, claiming that when Tybalt arrived Romeo "spoke him fair". The adjective "fair" suggests that Romeo speaks in a polite way to try to calm the situation. Benvolio therefore presents Romeo as fundamentally peaceful despite his later actions, which shows Benvolio's loyalty. The importance of loyalty to Benvolio reflects the fact that honour and family were strong influences on life in Italy at the time the play is set.

• Benvolio is presented as intelligent. In the extract, Benvolio structures his account in a way which makes the Prince sympathetic to Romeo, stating "There lies the man, slain by young Romeo, / That slew thy kinsman, brave Mercutio." Benvolio makes Tybalt the subject of the sentence, which suggests that he is the answer to the Prince's request to know who started the fight. This shows that Benvolio can think quickly to make the best of a situation. Benvolio's intelligence is emphasised by the fact that his description of Romeo's attempt to keep the peace occupies more lines in his account than his description of Romeo killing Tybalt. This also makes Romeo seem less responsible for the fight.

• Elsewhere in the play, Benvolio is presented as peaceful. In Act 1, Scene 1, he urges the servants to "Part, fools!" and stop fighting. Benvolio rarely uses insulting language, so the fact that he calls the servants 'fools' indicates how strongly he wants the fight to end, showing his peaceful nature. The strength of Benvolio's wish to end the violence is indicated by the stage directions, which state that he "*Beats down their swords*", suggesting Benvolio will go to great lengths to maintain peace.

4. a) • Juliet is presented as a determined character in the extract by her refusal to leave the tomb. Her determination to remain is highlighted by the words "stay" and "away". These words are opposites of each other, which shows that Juliet wants to do exactly the opposite of what Friar Lawrence tells her to. Juliet's determination is emphasised when she rejects the Friar's offer to send her to "a sisterhood of holy nuns". He is offering her an escape from death but she would still rather remain in the tomb.

• Shakespeare also presents Juliet as determined through her suicide. She says that the dagger should "rust" in her body, a process that takes a long time. This shows that she embraces the permanence of her decision to die. The strength of her determination to die is emphasised by the fact that religious rules at the time Shakespeare was writing stated that suicide was a sin. An audience at the time would therefore have understood that Juliet is so determined to die, she is willing to go to hell.

• Juliet is presented as determined through the way she behaves decisively in this scene. She searches for a way to kill herself, trying to poison herself by kissing Romeo, then taking his dagger to stab herself. The fact that she is so decisive, despite her grief, shows how determined she is to die. Her decisive behaviour is highlighted by her positive language in this extract, calling a drop of poison "friendly" and the poison itself a "restorative". These contrasting ideas suggests that her determination to die is so strong, she can only see positivity in death.

b) • Sin is significant as it influences Juliet's decisions in the play. Juliet decides to be faithful to Romeo rather than commit a sin by marrying Paris. She states that God joined her heart to Romeo's and thus marrying Paris would be a "treacherous revolt". This shows that she would not only be betraying Romeo if she married Paris, but also her religious values. A 16th-century audience would have understood the seriousness of Juliet's situation, as people believed they had to live by the moral rules of their religion, so risking death from the potion would have seemed preferable to committing such a serious sin.

• Sin is significant as it shows how extreme Romeo and Juliet's love is. For example, in Act 2, Scene 2, Juliet tells Romeo to "swear by thy gracious self, / Which is the god of my idolatry". Here Juliet compares her feelings for Romeo to the worship of a "god". It is a sin for Christians to worship false idols, so her use of the word "idolatry" shows that she realises the potentially sinful nature of their relationship. The implication of sin in this scene contrasts with Romeo and Juliet's first meeting, when they use religious imagery to show that they feel their love is sacred.

• Sin is significant as it influences Friar Lawrence's actions. In Act 2, Scene 6, Friar Lawrence says that he will marry Romeo and Juliet quickly because he doesn't want them to "stay alone" (sleep together) before they have been married. Most people at the time Shakespeare was writing believed that sex before marriage was a sin, so Friar Lawrence seems to be acting to prevent them from sinning. This scene is also very short, which gives it a frantic atmosphere. This suggests that Romeo and Juliet's relationship is out of control, giving weight to the Friar's fears that they might commit a sin.

The Characters from 'Romeo and Juliet'

After all those questions, you should be a *Romeo and Juliet* pro. Time to reward yourself with a little light relief. Find a comfy chair, put your feet up and feast your eyes on *Romeo and Juliet — The Cartoon*...

The Montagues

The Capulets

Romeo

Juliet

Montague and Lady Montague

Benvolio

Tybalt

Capulet and Lady Capulet

Other Characters

Count Paris

The Prince

Friar Lawrence

Nurse

Mercutio

William Shakespeare's 'Romeo and Juliet'